THE BEADED SPHERE
AND VARIATIONS

Judy Walker

Photography by
Richard Walker

Beading in the Third Dimension

Happy beading!

Judy Walker

WALKER PUBLICATIONS

www.walkerpublications.com

Text and diagrams copyright ©2008 by Judy Walker

Photography copyright ©2008 Richard Walker, except as noted below
    Dedication page: top photo ©2008 James Harrell
    Page 208: photos ©2008 Wendy Hubick
    Page 209: top photo ©2008 Birgit Bergemann
    Page 210: top photo ©2008 Sam Hay
    Page 210: middle and bottom photo ©2008 Ross Paxton
    Page 211: top right photo ©2008 Mark Dintenfass
    Page 214: top photo ©2008 Cathy Mykles

Design by Claudia Laub and Barbara Jefferies

ISBN 978-0-9816-553-7-6

Published by Walker Publications

www.walkerpublications.com

Printed in China

Dedication

This book is dedicated to the memory of my dear friend Penny Harrell. Having the good fortune to know Penny was a turning point in my life. She was a gifted artist and a lovely person in every way. Her support and enthusiasm helped me reach for things I never thought I could do. Everything I have ever accomplished as an artist is directly due to Penny's guidance and encouragement. I hope she'd be proud of this book. I'd give anything if I could show it to her.

Photo: James Harrell

Photo: Judy Walker

And this is also dedicated to my husband, Richard. Words can't express how much this book was a joint effort. My name may be on the cover, but Richard's good taste, suggestions, and expertise are all through it, as well as his beautiful photography. Even beyond that, though, his support and encouragement got me through times of self-doubt, and his help with my share of the more mundane parts of life—like housework, meals, errands, and cat boxes—made it possible for me to write this book.

Three Ivory Spheres, page 85

Chain Maille Necklace, page 193

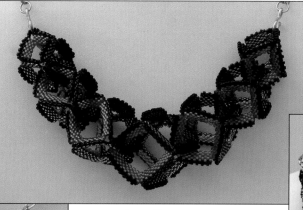

Seven Cubes Necklace, page 163

Stars and Stripes Forever, page 101

Byzantine Chain Necklace, page 185

*Seven Cubes Necklace,
page 163*

Mystery Weave Bracelet, page 135

Pinched Cube Chain Necklace, page 175

Star Sphere, page 79

Entangled Cubes Necklace, page 151

Rainbow Sphere, page 93

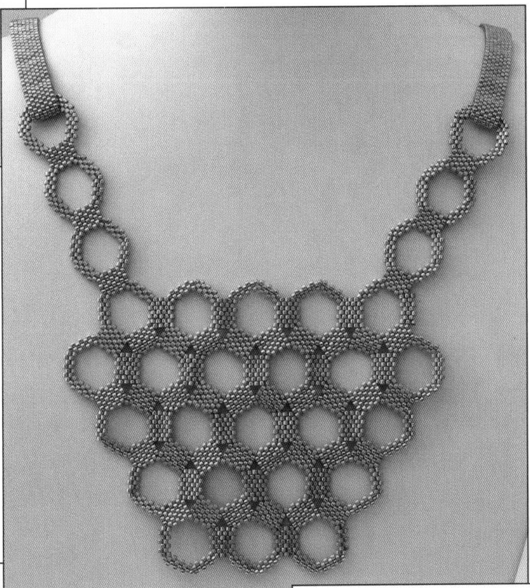

Honeycomb Necklace, page 75

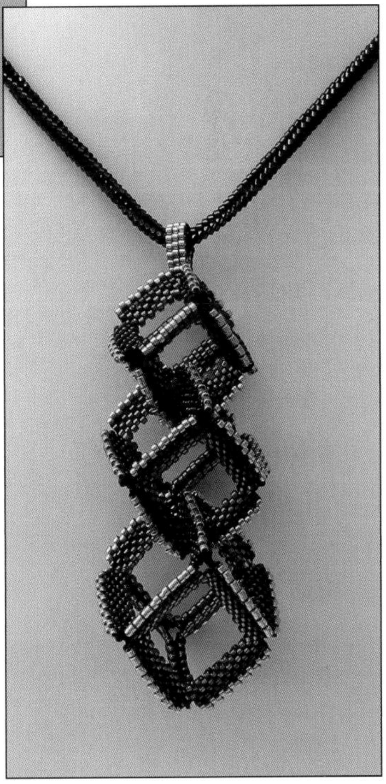

Entangled Cubes Necklace, page 151

Octagon Sphere, page 109

Entangled Spheres, page 123

Table of Contents

How to Use This Book 1

Information About Materials 2

Part One: The Basics 3

   The First Basic Shape—a Hexagon 4

   Sewing in Threads and Trimming Them Short 13

   Joining Shapes with Four Rounds 15

   Beading a "Spine" Where the Shapes Join 17

   Joining Shapes with Three Rounds 21

Part Two: Variations 23

   Making Different Shapes 24

   Making Different Sizes 27

   Filled Shapes 31

   Turning Shapes into Stars 39

   Acute Angles—Triangles 47

   Extremely Obtuse Angles 51

   Extra Rows Around the Edge 54

   Non-Regular Shapes 58

   Linking and Entangling Shapes 65

   Pinching and Attaching Shapes 69

Part Three: Projects 73

   Honeycomb Necklace 75

Table of Contents

Star Sphere 79

Three Ivory Spheres 85

Rainbow Sphere 93

Stars and Stripes Forever 101

Octagon Sphere 109

Entangled Spheres 123

Mystery Weave Bracelet 135

Entangled Cubes Necklace 151

Seven Cubes Necklace 163

Pinched Cube Chain Necklace 175

Byzantine Chain Necklace 185

Chain Maille Necklace 193

Sphere Assembly 201

Part Four: The Gallery 207

Part Five: Additional Information 221

Stitch Reference 222

Resources 227

A Few Words on Copyright 228

Afterword 229

About the Author 230

About the Photographer 231

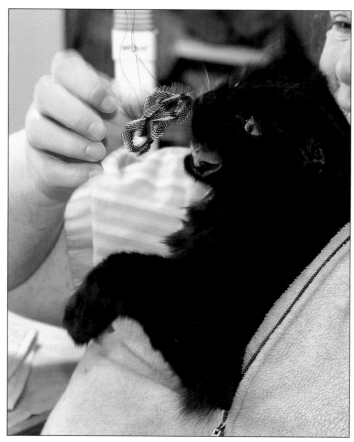

Some days it's a miracle that anything gets accomplished.

How to Use This Book

Everything in this book derives from one simple concept—a method of beading shapes and joining them together. I've described these basic techniques step by step in Part One. Before you tackle anything else, please work through Part One and learn these basics, because they apply to everything else in the book.

In Part Two, I teach you ways to change these basic techniques to produce different effects. Each of these variations stands alone—you don't have to go through them in order. Once you've learned the techniques in Part One, you can go directly to any variation you're interested in. A mind-boggling array of possible designs can be made with these variations, and you'll be able to create your own designs with this information.

In Part Three, I give directions for thirteen different projects using these techniques. Each project uses one or more of the variations in Part Two, and refers back to these instructions. Each project stands alone—once you've learned the techniques in Part One, you can go directly to the project you are interested in.

Part Four is a Gallery of original designs that other bead artists have come up with using these techniques. Some of these artists were students of mine, and there is nothing more rewarding for a teacher than to see an idea taken further than she ever imagined. Seeing all this beautiful beadwork was an enormous thrill, and made me realize that my designs barely scratch the surface of all the different possibilities of these techniques.

Send a picture of your original designs made from these techniques to the email link on my website at www.walkerpublications.com. I'll have a Gallery section online to share them with everyone.

Part Five contains some reference information about basic beading stitches and sources for materials.

Information About Materials

All of these designs were made using cylinder beads. Cylinder beads are straight-sided beads, shaped like a can of tuna. (Seed beads, another type, are round-sided and shaped like a donut.) The most common types of cylinder beads are Delicas, made by Miyuki, and Treasures or Aikos, made by Toho. Also available are Magnificas, distributed by Mill Hill. For many years, cylinder beads were made in one size, sometimes called 11/0, although they are slightly smaller than a typical size 11/0 seed bead. These are the cylinder beads I use in almost all the projects in this book.

All these beads—11/0 Delicas, Magnificas, Treasures, and Aikos—are the same size and can be used interchangeably in any of these designs. Mixing the brands of beads gives you a huge color palette to select from.

Recently, other sizes of cylinder beads have begun to be available. Miyuki makes several sizes of Delica beads, from large 8/0s to tiny 15/0s.

Delicas, Treasures, and Magnificas are excellent beads and a pleasure to work with. You'll find some misshapen or non–standard–sized beads as you work, and be sure to discard them. The more carefully you cull these cylinder beads, using only the best-shaped and most uniform ones, the more precise and even your finished beadwork will look.

Aikos are the highest quality of cylinder bead available, with virtually no misshapen or non–standard–sized beads. I have used Aikos for years, and they are my absolute favorite. The precision of Aiko beads saves me a lot of time, as I don't have to examine each one before I use it, and I don't have to pick out and redo beadwork to get rid of a misshapen bead I missed. Aikos have larger holes than other cylinder beads, so they allow more thread passes, and there are more Aiko beads per gram.

Many fine beading threads are available. My favorite thread is Nymo. I usually use size B or D for these designs. I also like KO thread. Any beading thread you like can be used, although if you use a thread that is thicker than Nymo D, you may find that your bead holes become too full in places where you need to make many passes through the same bead. I don't believe these designs need the strength of the extra-strong beading threads like Power Pro or Fireline.

The Basics

The First Basic Shape—a Hexagon

Let's make a beaded shape—a six-sided shape called a hexagon. We'll talk about different sizes and shapes and lots of other variations later, but you'll be using the same basic techniques for all of them.

ROUND ONE
Use a thread about three feet long, and don't double it. You won't need a stopper bead or a knot.

Start by picking up 36 beads.

Pass your needle through all 36 beads again to form a circle. Continue on through a few more beads (it doesn't matter how many) so that your needle is coming out of a different place than your tail.

Leave a tail long enough to sew back in later—about six or eight inches. You should be beading with a firm, but not tight, tension.

In these illustrations, Round One beads are shown in red.

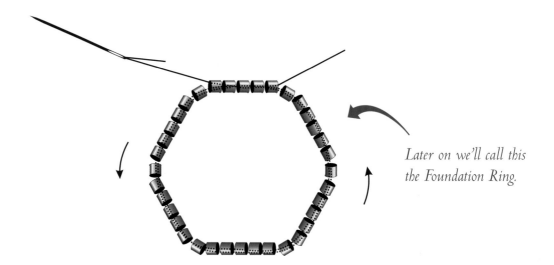

Later on we'll call this the Foundation Ring.

ROUND TWO

For the first stitch of Round Two, pick up two beads, skip one bead in your circle, and stitch through the next bead in the circle. In these illustrations, Round Two beads are shown in yellow.

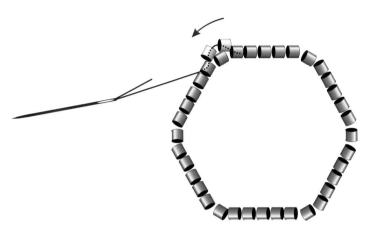

For the second stitch of Round Two, pick up one bead, skip one bead in your circle, and stitch through the next bead in the circle.

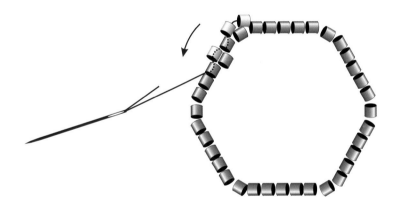

For the third stitch of Round Two, pick up one bead, skip one bead in your circle, and stitch through the next bead in the circle.

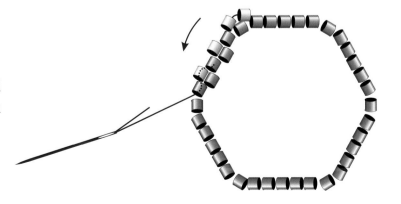

6

Continue stitching all the way around the circle in this same pattern—add two beads, add one bead, add one bead—skipping one bead in the circle each time.

Make sure, when you add the last bead of Round Two, that you stitch through a bead on the original circle.

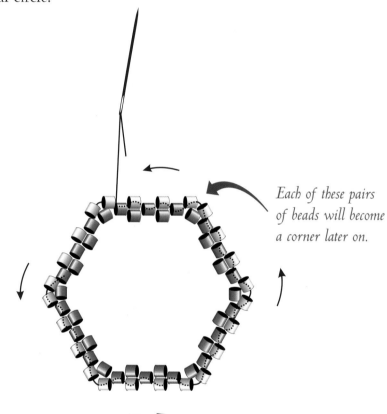

Each of these pairs of beads will become a corner later on.

"Step up" to the next round by stitching through the first two beads you added in Round Two.

Notice that there are two single-bead stitches between the pairs.

ROUND THREE
After you finish Round Two and do the "step up," your needle is coming out of the first two beads that were added in Round Two. Pick up one bead on your needle, and stitch through the next "sticking-up" bead—a single bead from Round Two. In these illustrations, the Round Three beads are shown in green.

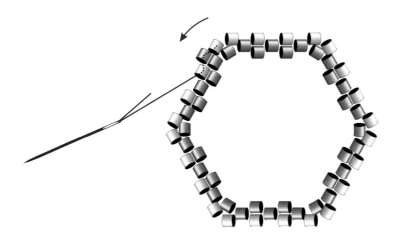

Pick up one more bead on your needle and stitch through the next "sticking-up" bead—another single bead from Round Two.

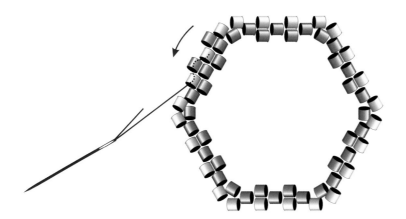

Pick up one more single bead on your needle and stitch through the next two sticking-up beads—the two beads from Round Two. Stitch through both of them.

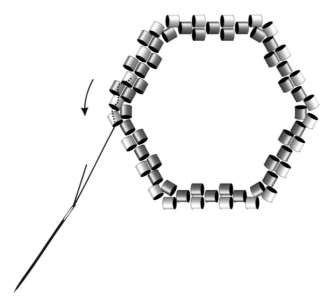

Continue stitching around the circle, adding one bead at a time. In this round, when you come to two beads, stitch through both of them as if they were one bead—**except for the last stitch.**

When you add the last bead of Round Three, stitch through only one of the two sticking-up beads from Round Two. Your needle will come out between these two beads. Do not step up at the end of Round Three.

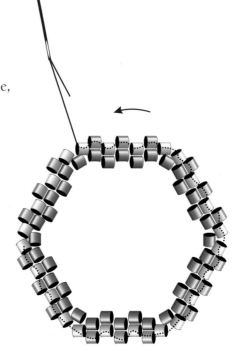

ROUND FOUR

In Round Four, we are going to make six little separate sides. These sides will be four beads wide. The pairs of beads from Round Two will be the corners of the hexagon. Each bead of the pair belongs to a different side. In these illustrations, Round Four beads are shown in blue.

Your needle is coming out between the two beads of a pair. In the first three rounds, you have been beading in the same direction—counter-clockwise around and around the circle. To start Round Four, you are going to change direction and bead in the opposite direction—clockwise.

Pick up one bead on your needle and stitch back into the last bead you added in Round Three.

Make two more stitches, adding a single bead each time, in this same direction.

The fourth and last bead of the side will sit on top of the first bead of the pair from Round Two.

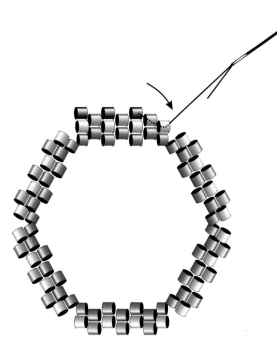

Stitch down through the first bead of the pair, coming out between the two beads of the pair.

Pick up one bead on your needle and change direction again, stitching into the last Round Three bead you just came out of.

This finishes off one of the four-bead-wide sides. When you bead firmly, with gentle tension, the sides will align into straight lines. Continue making these Round Four sides all the way around the hexagon.

To start the next side, you have to "travel" your needle until it is in the right spot to start beading. You want your needle to come out between the two beads of the pair, coming out of the bead that does not have a Round Four bead on top of it.

Here are detailed illustrations of the thread path you will use to "travel" the needle to the correct place to start the next side.

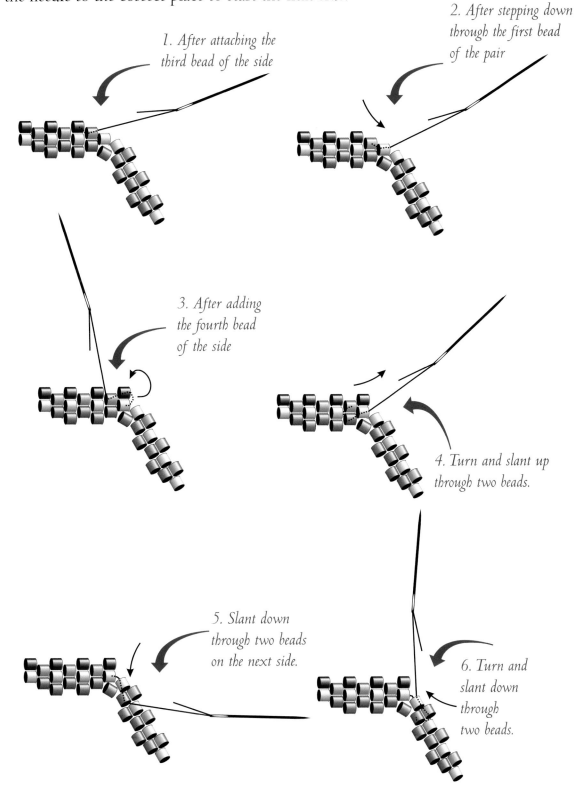

1. After attaching the third bead of the side

2. After stepping down through the first bead of the pair

3. After adding the fourth bead of the side

4. Turn and slant up through two beads.

5. Slant down through two beads on the next side.

6. Turn and slant down through two beads.

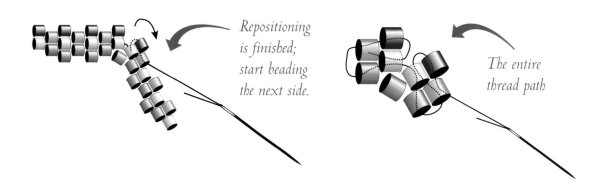

Repositioning is finished; start beading the next side.

The entire thread path

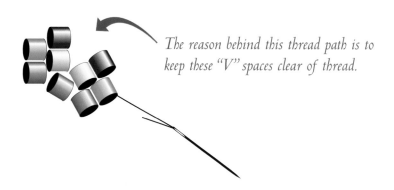

The reason behind this thread path is to keep these "V" spaces clear of thread.

This completes the first shape—a hexagon. You can sew in your tail thread securely and trim it short. In most cases, you'll use the rest of the working thread to join shapes together, but for your first shape, just sew in your working thread and trim it short.

Sewing in Threads and Trimming Them Short

When you sew in threads, you don't want them to come loose, and you don't want the little short trimmed ends to show on your beadwork. In some beadwork, especially flexible items that will move and twist a lot, I like to use several knots to secure my threads. However, knots can sometimes be visible, so when I am beading rigid structured items like these shapes, I don't use them.

I find that stitching through several beads at a time in three directions and crossing the thread path at least once does a great job of securing the thread on non-flexible beadwork. The thread path can be anything you want, as long as you never stitch on top of beads. You always want your thread to be hidden!

Here's an example of stitching through beads in three directions:

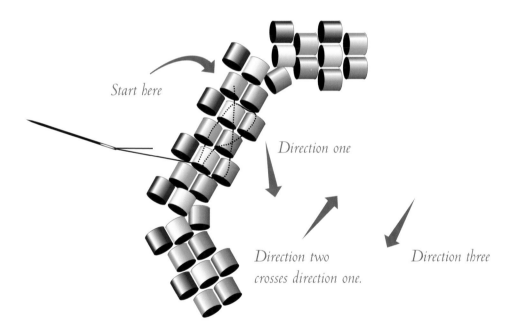

Start here

Direction one

Direction two crosses direction one.

Direction three

I try to avoid using the outermost beads, since I'll be stitching through them to join the shapes later, and any more stitching can pull out thread ends.

To cut off a thread, I pull it tightly, stretching it a little bit, and then cut it off with my scissor blades parallel to the beadwork. Never cut down into beadwork with the tips of your scissors—you might cut something you wish you hadn't!

When you stretch a thread a little bit before you cut it, the cut end pulls back inside the last bead, and you don't end up with short fuzzy ends showing.

Inexpensive acrylic frames do a great job of protecting beadwork in progress from natural disasters.

Joining Shapes with Four Rounds

After you have made your first basic shape, and sewed in and trimmed both the tail thread and the working thread, make a second shape. This can be any shape you want, as long as there are the same number of beads on each side as the first shape. For the examples here, I'll show you how to join two hexagons. We'll talk about other variations later.

When you have finished beading your second hexagon, sew in and trim your tail thread, but not your working thread. You'll be using it to join the two shapes.

Travel your needle until it is coming out one of the corner beads from Round Four, facing the rest of the side.

Add three single beads to form a "Joining Row." These beads fill in the gaps when you put the two shapes together. In these illustrations, the Joining Row beads are shown in purple.

Stitch in a loop around the bead just below
the Round Four bead you are coming out of,
to lock the last Joining Row bead firmly in place.

Turn and stitch into
the corner bead
of the first hexagon.

Zig-zag through the beads,
alternating stitching through
a bead from the Joining Row
and a bead from the first hexagon.

Turn and zig-zag back, alternating stitching through a bead from the second hexagon and a bead from the Joining Row.

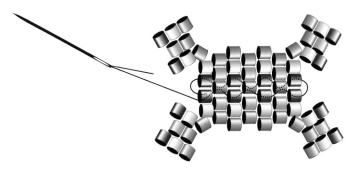

If you are joining shapes to make a flat beaded surface, this is all you need to do. You can sew in and trim your working thread. If you are joining shapes to make a larger three-dimensional object, you will need to bead a "Spine" where the shapes join, which will stiffen the beadwork.

Beading a "Spine" Where the Shapes Join

The Spine of beads that stiffens the shapes where they are joined is beaded on top of the surface.

Notice that there are two corner Round Four beads right next to each other, and your needle is coming out of one of them. In this illustration, it is the lower of the two corner Round Four beads.

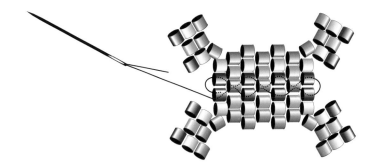

Pick up one Spine bead and stitch into the next Joining Row bead. In these illustrations, the Spine beads are shown in gray.

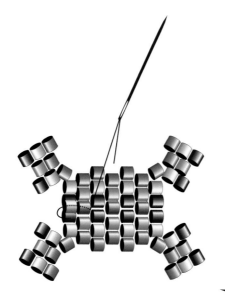

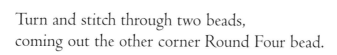

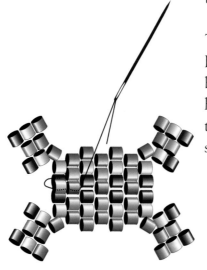

Turn and stitch through two beads, coming out the other corner Round Four bead.

Turn and stitch through the Spine bead and through the Joining Row bead.

This attaches the Spine bead to both of the corner Round Four beads, and causes it to sit straight between them in the "valley." Without the second half of this attachment, the Spine bead would tend to sit crookedly on top of the join, and the joined shapes would not be as strong and rigid.

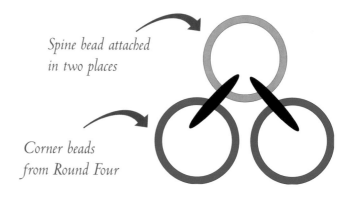

Spine bead attached in two places

Corner beads from Round Four

The next two Spine beads can be attached in a straight line—they do not need two attachment points. Stitch through Joining Row beads to attach these two Spine beads. The Spine beads sit in the "valleys" between two Round Four beads.

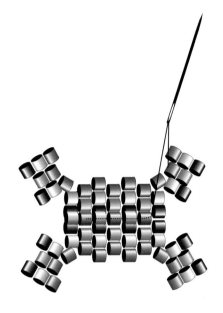

The last Spine bead is attached in the same way as the first one. It needs two attachment points to be strong and to sit straight between the two corner Round Four beads.

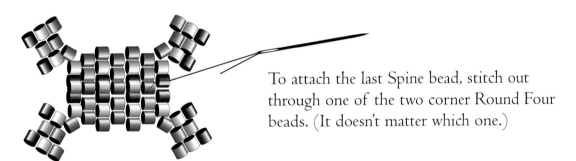

To attach the last Spine bead, stitch out through one of the two corner Round Four beads. (It doesn't matter which one.)

Pick up one Spine bead and turn and stitch through the nearest Joining Row bead.

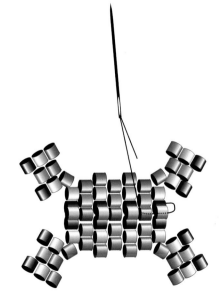

Turn and stitch through two beads, coming out the **other** corner Round Four bead.

Turn and stitch through the Spine bead.

Complete the Spine by beading
three more single beads, one
at a time, stitching through
the previous Spine beads.

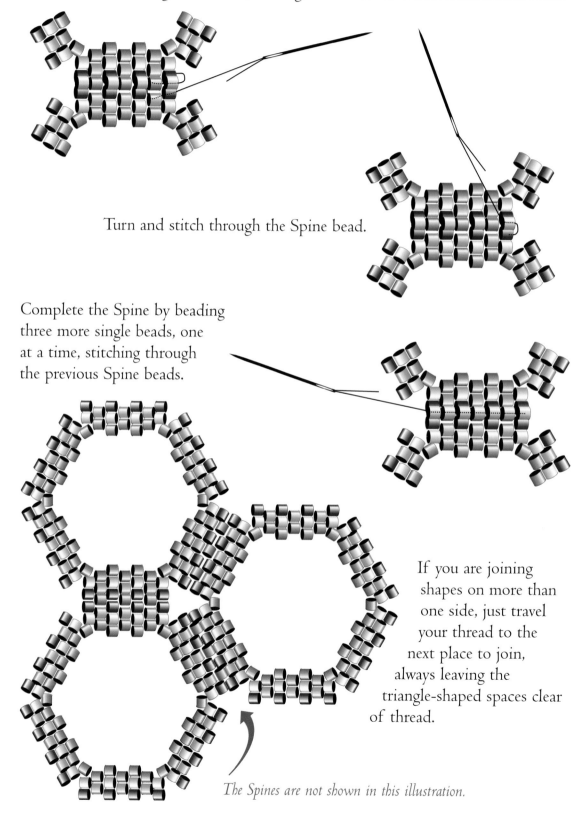

If you are joining
shapes on more than
one side, just travel
your thread to the
next place to join,
always leaving the
triangle-shaped spaces clear
of thread.

The Spines are not shown in this illustration.

Joining Shapes with Three Rounds

To create a different effect, you can also join shapes after only three rounds. Any two shapes with the same number of beads on each side can be joined. In this example, I'll show you how to join two hexagons.

Bead a hexagon as described on page 4, but **do not** bead Round Four. Stop after Round Three.

This is where the needle will come out after you attach the last Round Four bead that is used for a Joining Row.

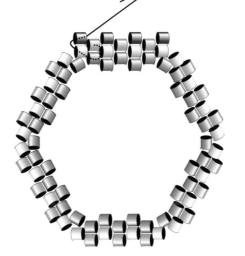

Bead a second identical hexagon. Bead **one side** of Round Four beads. These beads will be used as a Joining Row.

Reposition your needle so it is coming out one of the corner beads from the single Round Four side, facing the rest of the side.

Position the first hexagon so three single stitches from Round Three (the stitches between the pairs of beads that form the corners) fit into the three spaces between the single side of Round Four beads on the second hexagon. Zig-zag through the beads, alternating stitching through a bead from the single Round Four side and a bead from Round Three of the first hexagon.

Turn and zig-zag back, alternating stitching through a bead from Round Three of the first hexagon and a bead from the single Round Four side.

I don't usually bead a Spine on top of shapes joined at Round Three. To bead a Spine in the center of these two shapes, on top of the Joining Row, secure the beads on the outside edge (the ones that need two attachment points each) in the second row of the Spine.

Making Different Shapes

So far, we have been making six-sided shapes, or hexagons, but these beaded shapes aren't limited to hexagons—they can have any number of sides. Two things determine the number of sides. One is the number of beads in Round One, which we call the Foundation Ring. The other is the number of stitches using single beads that you take between the two-bead stitches that form corners.

To make a six-sided hexagon, we start with a number of beads in Round One that is a multiple of twelve. That means twelve times some number is the number of beads we want for Round One. On page 4, we used twelve times three, or 36 beads. Think of twelve as the **Base Number**, and three as the **Multiple**. We'll refer to these terms again later.

To make a five-sided shape (a pentagon) we start with a number of beads that is a Multiple of ten. For this example, we'll use ten times three, or 30 beads. For this shape, ten is the Base Number, and three is the Multiple.

Start Round One by picking up 30 beads.
Double-check your count before you proceed.

Form a ring by stitching through all 30 beads, and then stitching through a few more so your needle is coming out in a different place than your tail. Leave a tail long enough to sew back in later—about six or eight inches.

Bead Round Two as detailed on page 5—
beading two beads, one bead, one bead,
repeating all the way around.
Step up through the first
pair of beads you added
in Round Two.

Because you started with fewer beads
in Round One, there are only five pairs of beads
forming five corners.

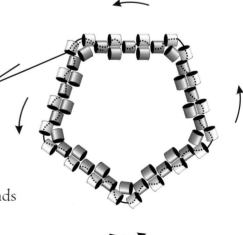

Continue beading Round Three and Round Four as you learned on pages 7–12.

Hey! This shape has four beads on each finished side, just like the hexagon from before!

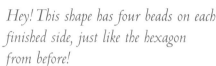

Notice that the five-sided pentagon has four beads on each finished side, just like the six-sided hexagon. This is because we used the same **Multiple** (three) for both shapes. The six-sided hexagon used twelve times three beads for Round One, and the five-sided pentagon used ten times three beads for Round One.

Different shapes can be joined together if they have the same number of beads on each finished side. Shapes made with the same Multiple always have the same number of beads on each finished side.

To make any shape, you need to know how many beads to pick up for Round One. You need a Base Number and a Multiple. **The Base Number is always going to be two times the number of sides you want.** For six sides, the Base Number is two times six, or twelve. For five sides, the Base Number is two times five, or ten. If you wanted a four-sided square, your Base Number would be two times four, or eight.

If you use the same Multiple each time, the different shapes will have the same number of beads on each finished side, and they can be joined together. A square that will have four beads on each finished side starts with a Base Number of eight, and a Multiple of three (the same Multiple we used for the hexagon on page 4 and the pentagon earlier in this part). Eight times three is 24. You would pick up 24 beads in Round One to make a square with four beads on each finished side.

This method of creating different shapes works for everything **except** triangles. For triangles, use the slightly different method described on page 47.

Shapes with eight or more sides have a tendency to distort and twist. Beading with less tension helps this. There is a variation in the way to figure out the number of beads in Round One, and to bead Round Two, that also produces a flatter, less twisted shape. This variation is described on page 51.

Amanda wants a dish of beads for a pillow, too!

Making Different Sizes

So far, we have been making different shapes with the same Multiple, so they have the same number of beads on each finished side. Our hexagon from page 4 used a Base Number of twelve and a Multiple of three, requiring 36 beads in the Foundation Ring. It had four beads on each finished side.

Using a different Multiple produces shapes in different sizes. When a different Multiple is used, Round Two will be slightly different. For a six-sided hexagon, there will always be six sides and six corners, no matter how big it is. In Round Two, the pairs of beads form the corners. You will need to figure out how many stitches of single beads there will be between the corners, so that the corners will be spaced evenly around the Foundation Ring. The bigger the shape, the more stitches of single beads there will be between each pair.

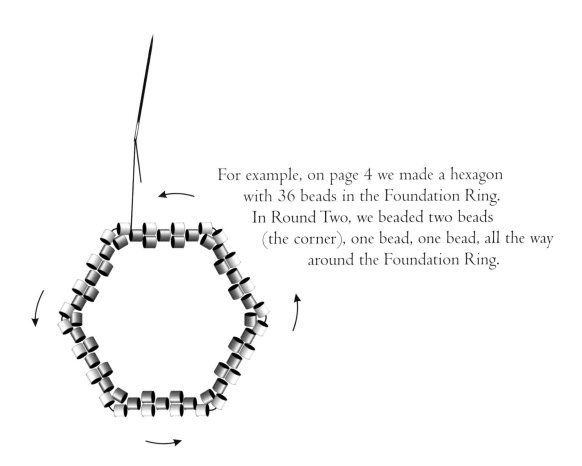

For example, on page 4 we made a hexagon
with 36 beads in the Foundation Ring.
In Round Two, we beaded two beads
(the corner), one bead, one bead, all the way
around the Foundation Ring.

To make a larger hexagon, we use a larger Multiple. If we choose four as the Multiple, we will have 48 beads in the Foundation Ring. (Hexagons always use a Base Number of twelve, and twelve times four equals 48.) But to space the pairs of beads evenly around the Foundation Ring, we would have to bead two beads, one bead, one bead, one bead, all the way around the Foundation Ring. In other words, there would be three stitches of single beads between each pair of beads.

Round Three and Round Four would be beaded the same way as before. Of course, there will be a few more stitches in each round. Notice that you end up with five beads on each finished side.

The hexagon made with a Multiple of three had two single beads between each pair in Round Two. It ended up with four beads on each finished side.

The hexagon made with a Multiple of four had three single beads between each pair in Round Two. It ended up with five beads on each finished side.

If you make other shapes using a Multiple of four, they will each have five beads on each side, and they can be joined together. All shapes made with the same Multiple always have the same number of beads on each finished side.

Calculating the Numbers

How Many Sides: Decide how many sides you want.

Base Number: Multiply the number of sides times two. For example, for a six-sided hexagon, the base number would be twelve.

Multiple: Decide how big the shape should be. The larger the Multiple, the larger the shape will be.

Foundation Ring: Multiply the Base Number times the Multiple to get the number of beads you pick up for Round One, the Foundation Ring. For example, for a hexagon with a Multiple of four, the Foundation Ring will have twelve times four beads, or 48 beads.

Number of Stitches of Single Beads Between Pairs in Round Two: Subtract one from the Multiple. For example, if you start with a Multiple of four, there will be three stitches of single beads between each pair in Round Two.

Number of Beads on Each Side when Finished: Add one to the Multiple. For example, if you start with a Multiple of four, there will be five beads on each side when you are finished with Round Four.

For a hexagon with a Multiple of four, you will start with 48 beads in the Foundation Ring. In this case, you will have three stitches of single beads between each pair in Round Two, and you will end up with five beads on each side when you are finished with Round Four.

For a hexagon with a Multiple of two, you will start with 24 beads in the Foundation Ring. In this case, you will have one single bead between each pair in Round Two, and you will end up with three beads on each side when you are finished with Round Four.

For a hexagon with a Multiple of one, you will start with 12 beads in the Foundation Ring. In this case, you will have no single bead between each pair in Round Two. Each stitch of Round Two will be a pair of beads. You will end up with two beads on each side when you are finished with Round Four. (Obviously, using a Multiple of one gives you the smallest shape you can make!)

The six hexagons below each used a different Multiple. From left to right, the Multiples were one, two, three, four, five, and six. The even-numbered sizes are used in the Three Ivory Spheres project, detailed on page 85.

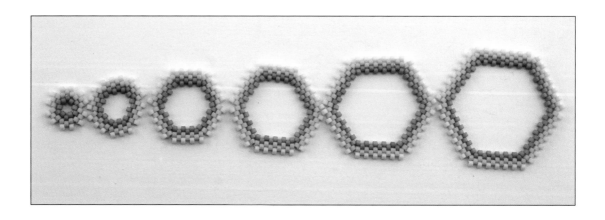

Filled Shapes

So far, we have been making hollow shapes like rings, with large openings in the middle. These openings can be filled in, making a solid shape.

Filled shapes are very similar to hollow shapes. You'll find the methods of beading the rounds very similar to the way you made the original shapes.

In this example, we'll make a filled hexagon that will be the same size as the hexagon on page 4—as if we had used a Multiple of three. There will be four beads on each finished side, and the filled hexagon can be joined to any other shape with a Multiple of three.

ROUND ONE
Start by picking up the same number of beads as the number of sides you want. In this example, for a hexagon, pick up six beads.

Pass your needle once more through all six beads to form a circle. Leave a tail long enough to stitch in later—about six or eight inches. Pass your needle through a few more beads so  your needle is not coming out of a bead right next to the tail. Leave your circle of beads a little loose, to allow room for the beads in the next round.

ROUND TWO
Add one bead between each bead from Round One. Each new bead you add in Round Two should sit between two of the beads from Round One. You can adjust the beads in your original circle if they are too tight. Step up by going through one more bead after you add the last bead.

ROUND THREE

Add two beads between each sticking-up bead from Round Two. At the end of this round, step up by going through the first two beads you added.

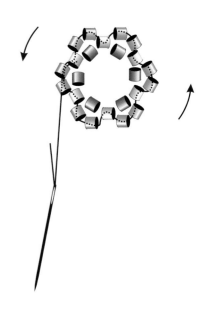

ROUND FOUR

Add one bead between each pair of sticking-up beads from Round Three. Do not step up at the end of this round— after adding the last bead, go through only one of the pair of beads.

ROUND FIVE

Pick up one bead. Double back and stitch through the sticking-up bead from Round Four and one bead of the next pair. Pick up one bead and double back again, stitching through the sticking-up bead and the bead you just came out of. Your thread path will be like a figure 8.

Pass your needle through three more beads—the next bead of the pair, the sticking-up bead, and the first bead of the next pair. This travels your needle forward to the correct position to start the next side.

This round forms two-bead-wide sides.

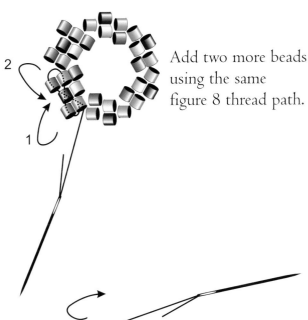

Add two more beads using the same figure 8 thread path.

Travel forward through three beads. Continue adding beads using this same figure 8 thread path until you have added six pairs of beads. Do not step up at the end of this round. Instead, turn and go through the bead directly on top of the first bead of the pair.

If you wanted a filled hexagon to match an open hexagon with two beads on a side (beaded with a Multiple of one), you would now be finished.

ROUND SIX

Add one bead between the two you added using the figure 8 stitch. Add two beads between the pairs of beads you added using the figure 8 stitch. The space where you add two beads is "V" shaped and wider. The two beads that you add in this round sit on top of the two beads from Round Three. You will stitch all the way around the outside of the hexagon.

Step up after you add the last pair of beads by going through the first bead you added.

ROUND SEVEN

Add one bead at a time all the way around the outside. When you come to a spot where two beads were added, stitch through both of them.

At the end of the round, do not step up. Stitch through only the first bead of the next pair.

ROUND EIGHT

You will be making a three-bead-wide side. Double back and add two beads, one at a time.

Stitch down through the next bead, the first bead of the pair. Double back and add one bead—the third bead of the side— on top of the bead you just came out of.

To start the next three-bead-wide side, you have to travel your needle until it is in the right spot to start beading. You want your needle to come out between the two beads of the pair, coming out of the bead that does not already have a Round Eight bead on top of it.

Use exactly the same thread path as you did on page 11. Here is a detailed illustration of the thread path you will use to travel the needle to the correct place to start the next side. It may look a little different because the needle is traveling counter-clockwise instead of clockwise, but you can turn the work over and work it clockwise.

Continue around the outside in this manner, making a total of six sides with three beads in each one.

When you have finished the sixth side, double back and stitch through the bead on top of the bead you just came out of.

If you wanted a filled hexagon to match an open hexagon with three beads on a side (beaded with a Multiple of two), you would now be finished.

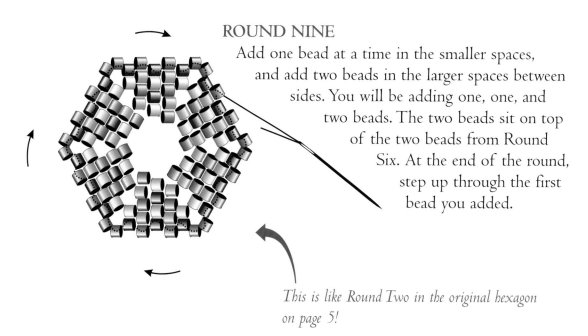

ROUND NINE

Add one bead at a time in the smaller spaces, and add two beads in the larger spaces between sides. You will be adding one, one, and two beads. The two beads sit on top of the two beads from Round Six. At the end of the round, step up through the first bead you added.

This is like Round Two in the original hexagon on page 5!

ROUND TEN

Add one bead at a time all the way around the outside. When you come to a spot where two beads were added, stitch through both of them.

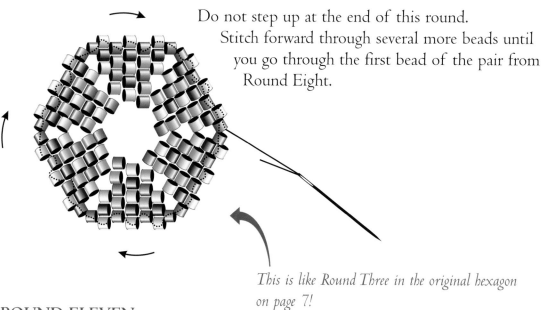

Do not step up at the end of this round. Stitch forward through several more beads until you go through the first bead of the pair from Round Eight.

This is like Round Three in the original hexagon on page 7!

ROUND ELEVEN

In Round Eleven, we are going to make six little separate sides. These sides will be four beads wide. These are identical to the sides we made in Round Four of the original hexagon on page 9.

Your needle is coming out between the two beads of a pair.
Pick up one bead on your needle, and
stitch back into the Round Ten bead.

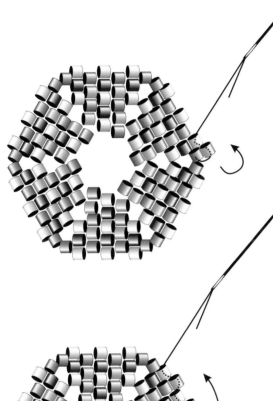

Make two more stitches, adding
a single bead each time, in this
same direction.

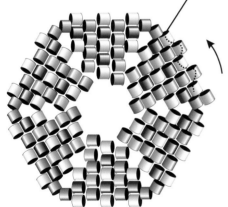

The fourth and last bead of the side will sit
on top of the first bead of the pair from
Round Nine.

Stitch down through the first bead of the pair,
coming out between the two beads of the pair.

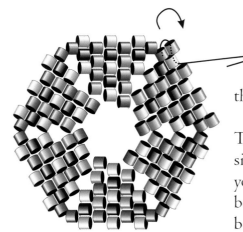

Pick up one bead on your needle, and change directions again, stitching into the last Round Nine bead you just came out of.

This finishes off one of the four-bead-wide sides. To start the next side, you have to travel your needle until it is in the right spot to start beading. You want your needle to come out between the two beads of the pair, coming out of the bead that does not have a Round Eleven bead on top of it.

Here is a detailed illustration of the thread path you will use to travel the needle to the correct place to start the next side.

This is identical to the method you used to bead Round Four of the basic hexagon on page 9. It may look a little different because the needle is traveling counterclockwise instead of clockwise, but you can turn the work over and work it clockwise.

If you wanted to make a larger filled hexagon, you would continue beading in the same way. The next round would be two beads in each corner, and single beads everywhere else. The next round after that would be single beads all the way around, going through the pairs of beads. The next round after that would build five-bead-wide sides in the same way as you built four-bead-wide sides in Round Eleven. Then you would repeat this sequence until the filled hexagon is as large as you want. Every three rounds, your finished sides would get one bead larger.

You can bead any shape as a filled shape using this same method. Just start the first round with the same number of beads as the number of sides you want.

Turning Shapes into Stars

These beaded shapes can be made into stars very easily. Six-sided hexagons and five-sided pentagons with a Multiple of three are especially easy, but any shape and any size can become a star.

You will need two different colors of beads to make a star. It is best if they have a strong contrast. We'll call them the Star Color and the Background Color. To make a six-sided star out of a hexagon with a Multiple of three, you will pick up 36 beads. Instead of picking them up all in one color, as in the example on page 4, you'll pick up a simple pattern.

ROUND ONE
Pick up 36 beads for the Foundation Ring in the following pattern:

> Two Star Color, one Background Color, two Star Color, one Background Color (etc.)

The last bead you pick up will be a Background Color, and there will be a total of twelve Background Color beads. Double-check your pattern and count the beads again before you proceed.

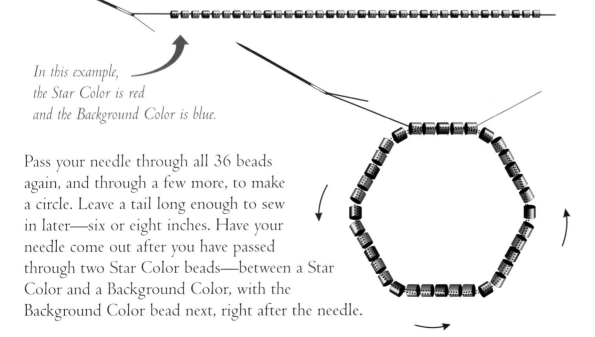

In this example, the Star Color is red and the Background Color is blue.

Pass your needle through all 36 beads again, and through a few more, to make a circle. Leave a tail long enough to sew in later—six or eight inches. Have your needle come out after you have passed through two Star Color beads—between a Star Color and a Background Color, with the Background Color bead next, right after the needle.

ROUND TWO
Pick up two Star Color beads, skip the Background Color bead in the circle, and stitch through one Star Color bead in the circle. The two Star Color beads you have added sit on top of the Background Color bead.

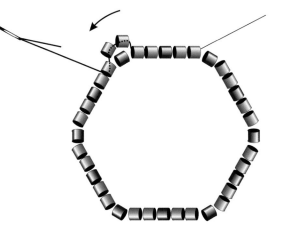

Pick up one Background Color bead, skip a bead in the circle (Star Color), and stitch through the next bead on the loop (Background Color).

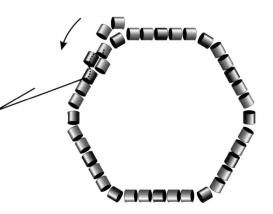

Pick up one Background Color bead, skip a bead in the circle (Star Color), and stitch through the next bead in the circle (Star Color).

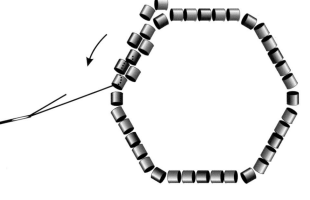

Continue in this pattern all the way around the circle: add two Star Color beads, one Background Color bead, one Background Color bead. You will do this a total of five more times to come around to the beginning of the circle. Step up to the next round by stitching through the first two beads you added in Round Two.

Two Star Color beads, forming the corners of the hexagon, always sit on top of a single Background Color bead. Single Background Color beads form a "V" with the Background Color bead in the circle.

Here's the "V" formed by the two single Background Color beads.

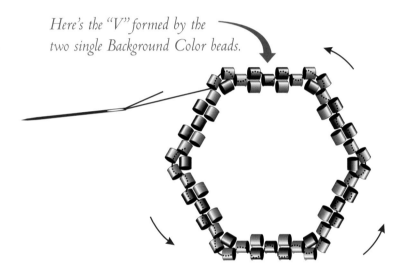

ROUND THREE

Bead around the hexagon, adding one bead at a time. Use all Background Color. In this round, when you come to two Star Color beads, stitch through both of them as if they were one bead—except for the last stitch.

When you add the last bead of Round Three, stitch through only one of the two Star Color beads from Round Two. Your needle will come out between these two beads. Do not step up at the end of Round Three.

ROUND THREE-AND-A-HALF—The Point of the Star

Pass your needle down through the next three Star Color beads, toward the center of the loop. Add one Star Color bead to complete the "V" shape, the point of the star. Pass your needle up through three Star Color beads.

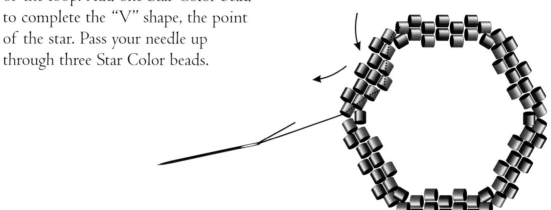

Continue around the inside of the hexagon, stitching through Star Color beads only, adding a single bead of Star Color at the bottom of each "V" to complete the points of the six-sided star shape. After you have added the last Star Color bead, pass your needle up through all three Star Color beads in a line, to come out between two Star Color beads.

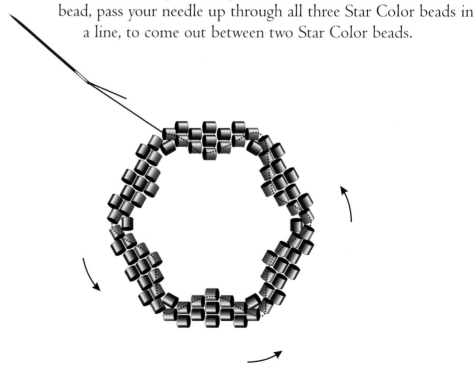

(Why is this called Round "Three-and-a-Half"? So that Round Four in this hexagon is the same as Round Four in the original example on page 9!)

ROUND FOUR

Bead Round Four the same way you did on the original hexagon on page 9.
Use all Background Color beads for this round.

Different Shapes of Stars Using a Multiple of Three

Different shapes of stars are beaded in the same way as this example. (See page 24 for information on beading different shapes.) Pick up the correct number of beads (Base Number times a Multiple of three) in the same pattern:

Two Star Color, one Background Color, two Star Color, one Background color (etc.)

Stars that are built
on a Multiple of three
need a single bead in
Round Three-and-a-
Half to complete
the star point. They
will all have four
beads on each
finished side.

Different Sizes of Stars—Multiple of Four

To make a larger star, with a larger Multiple, you would pick up a different pattern in Round One. For example, to make a six-sided hexagon with a Multiple of four into a star, pick up 48 beads in the following pattern:

Two Star Color, one Background Color, two Star Color, three Background Color, two Star Color, one Background Color, two Star Color, three Background Color (etc.)

Double-check your pattern and count the beads again before you proceed.

Form the Foundation Ring by passing your needle through all 48 beads, and then through some more beads. Come out after you pass through two Star Color beads, when the next bead in your circle is a **single** Background Color bead (not the first of three Background Color beads).

For Round Two, pick up two Star Color beads, skip the single Background Color bead, and stitch into a Star Color bead. Then bead three single beads of Background Color. Repeat all the way around the hexagon.

For Round Three, bead all the way around the hexagon using Background Color.

For Round Three-and-a-Half, you will have to add three Star Color beads to finish the point of the star. Pass around the inside of the hexagon, traveling through Star Color beads, and add two single stitches of Star Color beads to the point the first time around. Then pass around the inside of the hexagon again, traveling through Star Color beads, to add the single bead that completes the point.

For Round Four, you will make beaded sides that are five beads wide, using all Background Color.

Different Sizes of Stars—Multiple of Five

For a star hexagon with a Multiple of five, pick up 60 beads for the Foundation Ring in the following pattern:

Two Star Color, one Background Color, two Star Color, four Background Color, two Star Color, one Background Color, two Star Color, four Background Color (etc.)

Double-check your pattern and count the beads again before you proceed.

Form the Foundation Ring by passing your needle through all 60 beads, and then through some more beads. Come out after you pass through two Star Color beads, when the next bead in your circle is a **single** Background Color bead (not the first of four Background Color beads).

In Round Two, bead two Star Color beads on top of each **single** Background Color bead, then four single Background Color beads, all the way around.

For Round Three, bead all the way around the hexagon using Background Color.

Round Three-and-a-Half needs three times around the inside of the hexagon to complete the points of the star. The first time around, add three beads to each point: a Star Color, a Background Color, and a Star Color. The second time around, add two Star Color beads to each point. The third time around, add a single Star Color bead to each point.

For Round Four, you will make beaded sides that are six beads wide, using all Background Color.

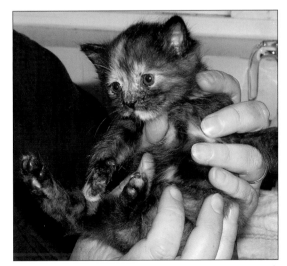

This little orphan found a good home after some tender bottle feeding by Judy!

Adjustments

Adjust the number of beads in the Foundation Ring according to the size and shape star you want, and adjust the pattern of beads you pick up in the Foundation Ring according to the pattern above.

You may find that your bead holes tend to fill up when you are beading larger stars that need a lot of passes around the inside to complete the star points. You may prefer to bead back and forth, beading one entire star point at a time by decreasing, and then traveling to the next spot.

Stars built on shapes with Multiples of two or one don't look like stars— a Multiple of three is the smallest star that looks good.

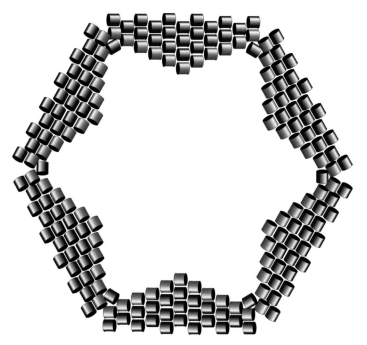

Acute Angles—Triangles

There are three kinds of angles: acute angles, right angles, and obtuse angles. Acute angles are smaller than right angles, and obtuse angles are larger than right angles.

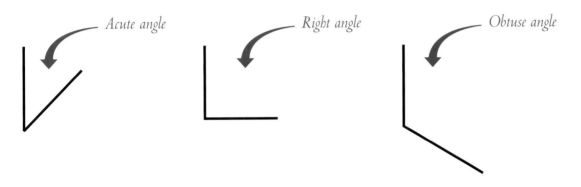

You can see that the angles of all kinds of shapes are either right angles or obtuse angles. These can all be beaded with the basic method of constructing shapes.

The basic method for making beaded shapes that I use in this book works well for all angles **except** acute angles.

You can see that the angles of all kinds of shapes are either right angles or obtuse angles. These can all be beaded with the basic method of constructing shapes.

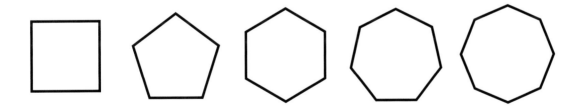

However, the angles of a triangle are acute angles.

Using the basic method for constructing a shape, which is detailed on page 24, you would expect that a triangle would have a Base Number of six (the three sides times two), multiplied by whatever Multiple you chose to use. For example, for a triangle with seven beads on each finished side, you'd have a Multiple of six. Base Number times Multiple equals 36, so you would expect to pick up 36 beads for your Foundation Ring.

But alas! This doesn't work as expected—the shape comes out twisted and distorted, and won't lie flat and cooperate with the other shapes. Triangles are very useful in all kinds of designs, and I was going crazy trying to figure out how to make triangles that worked with the other shapes I was beading. I was rescued by Juanita Quartullo, one of my students, who came up with this elegant method. Thanks for saving my sanity, Juanita!

Adjusting the Foundation Ring for Acute Angles

For each acute angle in a shape, you **subtract** one bead from the Foundation Ring number. In a triangle, there are three acute angles, so you subtract three beads from the number you calculate for the Foundation Ring.

In the example above, for a triangle with seven beads on each finished side, you'd have a Base Number of six and a Multiple of six. This comes out to 36 beads, and then you subtract three beads (one for each acute angle) from that number to get 33 beads for the Foundation Ring.

ROUND ONE
Pick up 33 beads for your Foundation Ring. Double-check your count before you proceed. Leave a tail long enough to sew back in later— about six or eight inches.

Pass your needle through all 33 beads again to form a circle. Continue on through a few more beads (it doesn't matter how many) so that your needle is coming out of a different place than your tail.

Round One always looks like a circle, but Round Two will turn it into a triangular shape.

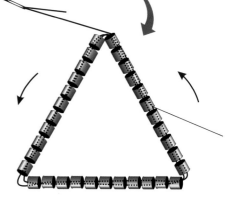

ROUND TWO

In all the other shapes, when you started Round Two, you picked up two beads that would form a corner, skipped one bead in the Foundation Ring, and then passed your needle through the next bead.

Instead, for an acute angle, you pick up two beads, but you **don't skip a bead.** Pass your needle into the very next bead in the Foundation Ring.

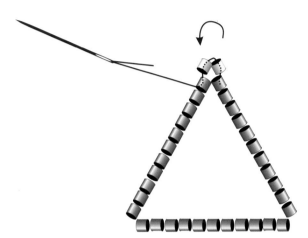

Bead five single beads. Remember that your Multiple is six, so the number of single-bead stitches between corners is one less than your Multiple.

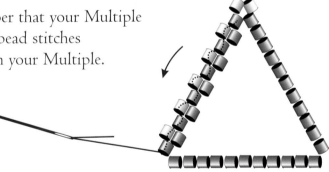

Pick up two beads and stitch into the very next bead in the Foundation Ring. Bead five more single beads, then bead another two beads without skipping a bead. Five more single beads will finish Round Two. Step up to the next round by passing your needle through the first two beads you added in Round Two.

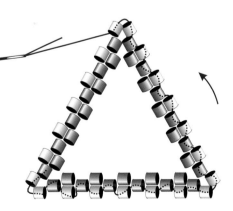

ROUND THREE

Bead all the way around the triangle,
one bead at a time. When you come
to two beads, pass your needle through
both of them. When you add the last bead
of Round Three, stitch through only one
of the two corner beads from Round Two.
Your needle will come out between these
two beads. Do not step up at the end
of Round Three.

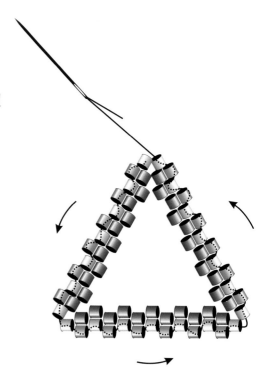

ROUND FOUR

Bead the sides of Round Four exactly the
same way as in the basic shape. (See page
9.) For this example, each finished side has
seven beads.

The method for beading shapes with acute
angles, such as triangles, is only a little bit
different than the basic method. Other
than adjusting the number of beads in the
Foundation Ring, and changing the way
you stitch the corners in Round Two,
everything else is the same.

Extremely Obtuse Angles

There are three kinds of angles: acute angles, right angles, and obtuse angles. Acute angles are smaller than right angles, and obtuse angles are larger than right angles. Only triangles have acute angles. The more sides a shape has, the more obtuse—the larger—its angles become.

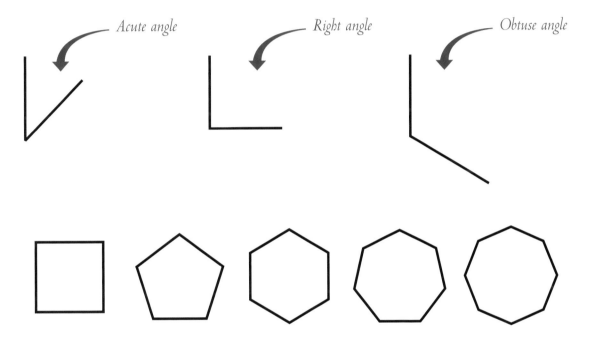

Acute angle   *Right angle*   *Obtuse angle*

Four-sided squares, five-sided pentagons, and six-sided hexagons work perfectly with the basic method of beading shapes. However, when you make seven-sided heptagons or eight-sided octagons (or shapes with even more sides) with the basic method, they can begin to twist and distort. The larger the shape you bead, the more chance there is for distortion.

There are several ways of dealing with this distortion. A shape with seven or more sides can be stabilized by other shapes joined around its edges. Another solution is beading with less tension.

A variation in the way you bead the corners can also help. For this example, we will make a large eight-sided octagon. Octagons use a Base Number of sixteen, and we will use a Multiple of five. This means there are 80 beads in the Foundation Ring, and four stitches of single beads between corner pairs.

To compensate and increase the shape's stability, we will **add** one bead to the Foundation Ring for each extremely obtuse angle. This adds eight beads to the Foundation Ring for a final total of 88 beads. Double-check your count before you proceed.

After forming Round One, pick up **three** beads for the first stitch, and stitch over **two** beads.

Bead four more single beads, then another corner of three beads, all the way around the Foundation Ring, forming eight sides and eight corners. Step up through all three beads at the end of Round Two.

For Round Three, pass through all three beads as you add single beads.

For Round Four, form your sides using the outer beads of each three-bead group, and ignore the middle bead.

Not every corner in a shape has to be beaded the same way. You can combine methods to give just enough ease from tension to allow a shape to lie flat. To each angle you compensate for, add one bead, and treat the corner as above. You could compensate for half the angles in a shape, and alternate beading the corners in the basic method and the compensated method above.

If, for example, you wanted to compensate for every other angle in a twelve-sided dodecagon (maybe for decorating the outside of a clock face?), you would add six beads to the Foundation Ring, and treat every other corner as above. Experiment to get the results you want!

The method for beading shapes with extremely obtuse angles, such as octagons, is only a little bit different than the basic method. Other than adjusting the number of beads in the Foundation Ring, changing the way you stitch the corners in Round Two, and ignoring the center bead of the corner in Round Four, everything else is the same.

"Wow, all that beading exhausted us—just had to take a nap!"

Extra Rows Around the Edge

You can make your shape thicker by beading extra rows around the outside edge. When shapes with extra rows are joined together, the small hole where the sides come together is larger, giving them a lacy look. There is room for two rows of Spine beads side by side if you like.

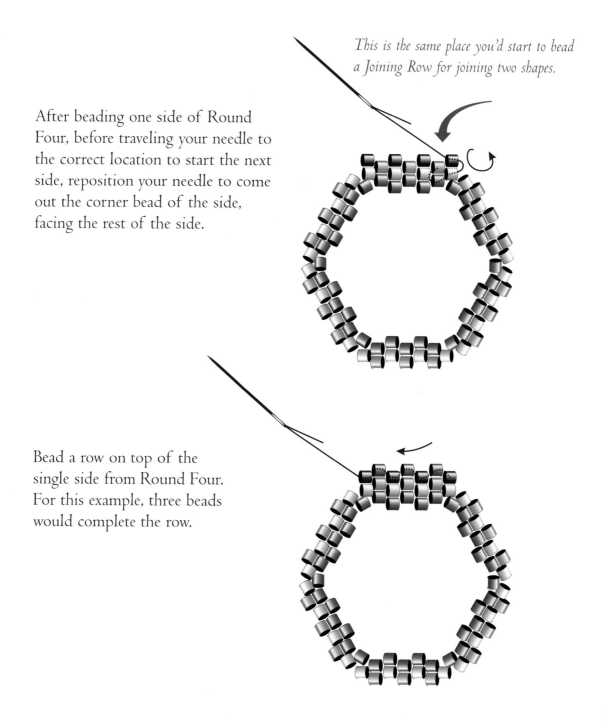

This is the same place you'd start to bead a Joining Row for joining two shapes.

After beading one side of Round Four, before traveling your needle to the correct location to start the next side, reposition your needle to come out the corner bead of the side, facing the rest of the side.

Bead a row on top of the single side from Round Four. For this example, three beads would complete the row.

Turn and bead three beads of a second row.

To attach the fourth and last bead of this
row, use the same method you used to
attach the fourth and last bead of each side
of Round Four.

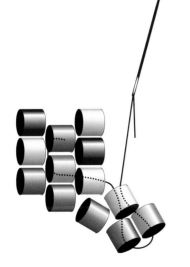

Travel your needle to the next position
for the next Round Four side.

When you join the sides of two shapes done in this manner, you can see that the triangular hole formed by the "V" shaped spaces between sides is larger.

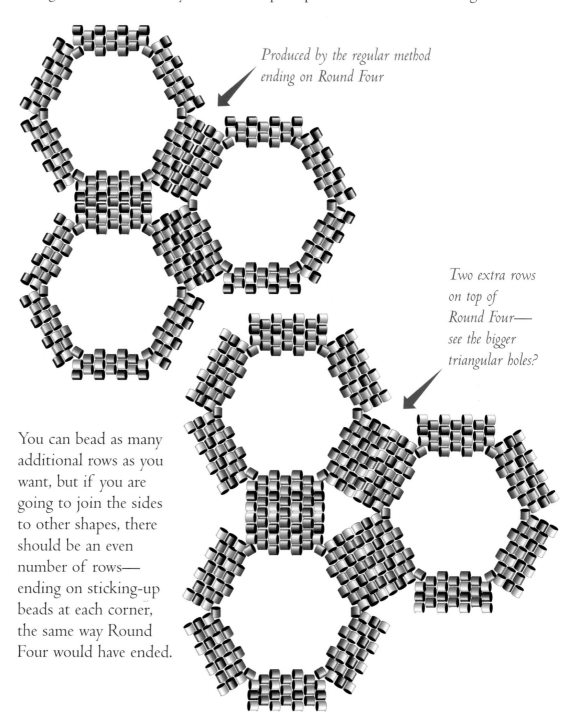

Produced by the regular method ending on Round Four

Two extra rows on top of Round Four— see the bigger triangular holes?

You can bead as many additional rows as you want, but if you are going to join the sides to other shapes, there should be an even number of rows— ending on sticking-up beads at each corner, the same way Round Four would have ended.

You can bead the sides into points by continuing to add rows and decreasing to a point. You will have to reposition your needle multiple times to get into position to add the next row. If you join shapes at their points only, they will be very flexible.

You may find the beadwork to be more flexible when you join shapes with extra rows. One row of Spine beads may not be enough. (See page 17 for more information on beading Spines.) If you need more rigidity, you can add two rows of Spine beads, one on either side of the Joining Row.

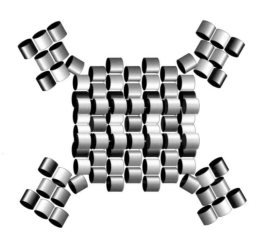

Non-Regular Shapes

So far, all the shapes we have been making have been **regular**—meaning that all the sides are the same length, **and** all the angles are the same.

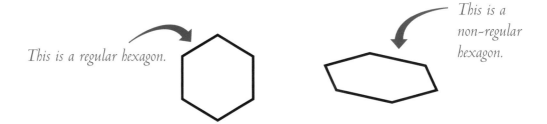

This is a regular hexagon.

This is a non-regular hexagon.

A square and a rectangle both have four sides, and both have four right angles. The square has all four sides the same length, and the rectangle has two sides longer than the other two. The square is a regular shape, and the rectangle is a non-regular shape.

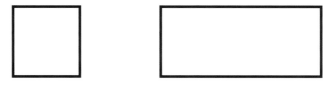

You can bead non-regular shapes by adjusting the number of beads in the Foundation Ring, and adjusting the number of single beads between corners in Round Two.

When we were calculating the number of beads in the Foundation Ring to bead a square with a Multiple of three, we multiplied the number of sides in a square (four) times two to get the Base Number of eight. Then we multiplied the Base Number times the Multiple of three to get 24 beads in the Foundation Ring.

Because the number of single beads between corners in Round Two is one less than the Multiple, we knew that there would be two single beads between the pairs of beads that formed corners when we beaded Round Two. We also knew that there would be four beads on each side when we were finished with Round Four, because the number of beads on each finished side is one larger than the Multiple.

To make a rectangle, you need to decide how many beads you want on the outside of each side when it is finished. For this example, let's say that the short sides will have four beads on each finished side, and the long sides will have eight beads on each finished side.

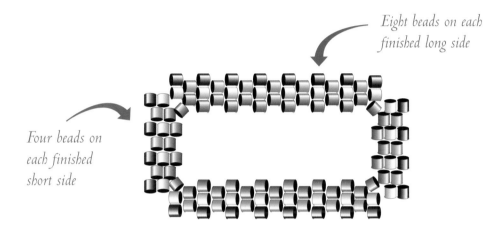

Eight beads on each finished long side

Four beads on each finished short side

The sides are different lengths, so we need to calculate how many beads we need for each separate side in the Foundation Ring.

First we figure out what the Multiple would have been if the shape had been a regular shape—a square—instead of a rectangle. For a square with four beads on each finished side, the Multiple would be three. For a square with eight beads on each finished side, the Multiple would be seven.

Each single side needs **twice** its Multiple of beads in the Foundation Ring. For the rectangle described above, a short side would have a Multiple of three, so it needs six beads in the Foundation Ring. The long side would have a Multiple of seven, so it needs fourteen beads in the Foundation Ring.

Going all the way around the rectangle, there's a short side, a long side, a short side, and a long side. So you'd need six plus fourteen plus six plus fourteen beads, or 40 beads, in the Foundation Ring to make the rectangle above.

For Round Two, you need to calculate how many single beads are stitched between the pairs of beads that form corners. In a regular shape, this would be the same number all the way around—one less than the Multiple.

If you were making a square with a Multiple of three, you would stitch a pair of beads for the corner, then a single bead, then a single bead, then a pair of beads for the corner. There would be two single stitches between each pair of beads that formed a corner.

If you were making a square with a Multiple of seven, there would be six single stitches between each pair of beads that formed a corner.

To make the rectangle described above, you'd stitch a pair of beads for a corner, then two single-bead stitches, then a pair of beads for a corner, then six single-bead stitches, then a pair of beads for a corner, then two single-bead stitches, then a pair of beads for a corner, then six single-bead stitches. (Remember to step up through the two corner beads at the end of Round Two.)

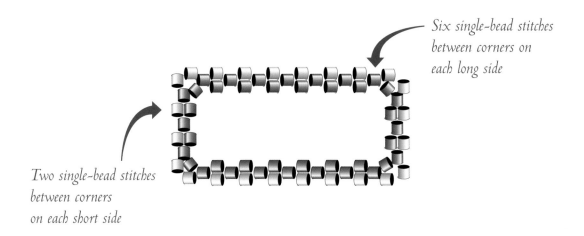

Six single-bead stitches between corners on each long side

Two single-bead stitches between corners on each short side

Round Three would be beaded in the same way as a regular shape.

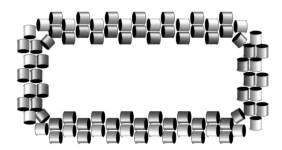

Round Four would be beaded in the same way as a regular shape.

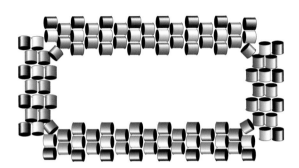

You can use this method to bead other non-regular shapes, too. Here is a non-regular hexagon that is stretched.

The top and bottom sides are longer than the other four sides.

Let's assume we want five beads on each finished shorter side, and eight beads on each finished longer side. Each short side would have a Multiple of four, and each long side would have a Multiple of seven.

You need twice the Multiple for **each** side in the Foundation Ring. For the six sides, you'd need eight plus eight plus fourteen plus eight plus eight plus fourteen beads, or a total of 60 beads in the Foundation Ring.

For Round Two, you'd bead a pair of beads for a corner, then three single-bead stitches, then a pair of beads for a corner, then three single-bead stitches, then a pair of beads for a corner, then six single-bead stitches, then a pair of beads for a corner, then three single-bead stitches, then a pair of beads for a corner, then three single-bead stitches, then a pair of beads for a corner, then six single-bead stitches. (Remember to step up through the two corner beads at the end of Round Two.)

Rounds Three and Four would be beaded in the same way as a regular shape.

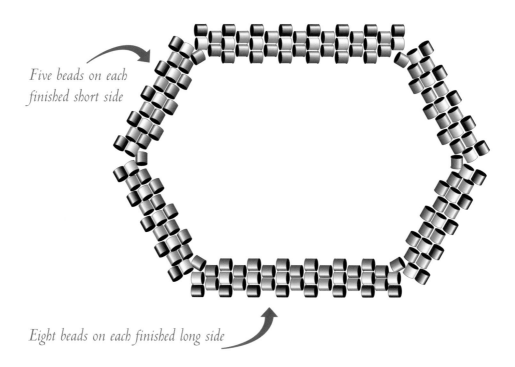

Five beads on each
finished short side

Eight beads on each finished long side

Another non-regular shape that can be beaded is a diamond.

Notice how a diamond differs from a square. It may have all four sides the same length, but the angles are different. Two of the angles are acute, or smaller than a right angle, and two of the angles are obtuse, or larger than a right angle. (A square's four angles are all the same—all right angles.)

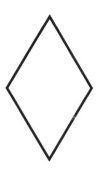

To make a diamond with five beads on each finished side, we need to use a Multiple of four. Each side would need twice the Multiple, or eight beads. You'd need eight plus eight plus eight plus eight, or 32 beads in the Foundation Ring.

But how is this different from a square? In a diamond, you also need to subtract two beads, one for each acute angle. (See page 47 for more information on acute angles.) This means there would be 30 beads in the Foundation Ring.

Round Two would have three single-bead stitches between each pair of beads that form a corner. However, every other corner would not skip a bead, to produce an acute angle. (It's not necessary to use the compensation method for extremely obtuse angles when beading the other two angles—they're not so obtuse as to cause distortion. Please see page 51 for more information on obtuse angles.)

Acute angle: don't skip a bead in Round One.

Obtuse angle: skip a bead in Round One as usual.

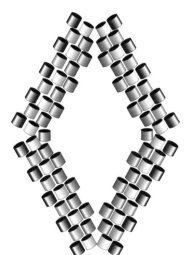

Rounds Three and Four would be beaded in the same way as a regular shape.

Some variations of shapes don't translate well into beads. When you are fitting non-regular shapes together like puzzle pieces—for example, to make a beaded representation of a quilt block—the precise shapes you need may not be achievable.

For example, if a triangle has one side that is three inches long, one side that is four inches long, and one side that is five inches long, a smaller version of the same shape can be beaded with three beads on one finished side, four beads on the next finished side, and five beads on the third finished side. (Not to get too technical, but a triangle with these measurements is a right triangle—one of the angles is a right angle.)

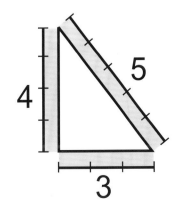

But if the triangle has one side that is three inches long, one side that is four inches long, and one side that is four-and-a-half inches long, it can't be beaded. This may not seem like much of a discrepancy, but it can make a big difference in how things fit together.

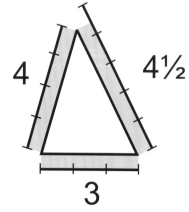

You should experiment to make sure your shapes fit together if you are planning a large project and using non-regular shapes. If you need a shape that is slightly non-regular—for example, the sides are all the same length, but the angles are slightly different—sometimes a beaded shape can be squished or deformed into the shape you need.

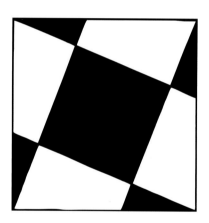
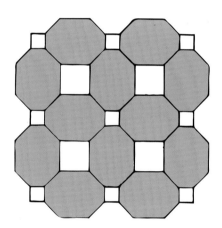

The left illustration, above, is a quilt block called Checkerboard Skew. It is an example of a quilt block with non-regular shapes that would be very difficult, if not impossible, to translate into beads. Although there is a regular square (in black) in the center, there are four non-regular four-sided shapes (in white) and four triangles (in black) that may not bead up into the right proportions to fit together.

The right illustration, above, is a quilt block called Octagon Tiles. It is an example of a quilt block with non-regular shapes that would translate very easily into beads. Notice that the octagons (eight-sided shapes, in gray) each have two short sides, where they touch the smaller squares, and six long sides, where they touch the larger squares and each other. To represent this quilt block in beads, you would bead non-regular octagons and regular squares, checking your proportions to make sure they fit together the way you want.

Linking and Entangling Shapes

Shapes can be linked together like a chain, or entangled together. I use the term "linking" when a shape is beaded through one other shape. I use the term "entangling" when a shape is beaded through two or more joined shapes.

To link two hexagons (six-sided shapes), construct the first hexagon as usual.

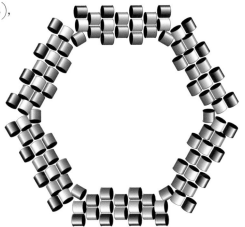

When you string the beads for the Foundation Ring of the second hexagon, pass your needle through the open center of the first hexagon as you form the Foundation Ring. Then pass your needle through all the beads of the Foundation Ring of the second hexagon, and a few more, passing through the open center of the first hexagon as needed. As you work, the first hexagon hangs from the Foundation Ring of the second hexagon.

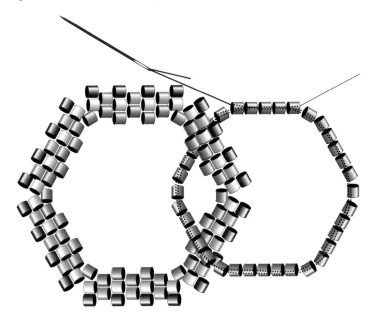

Continue constructing the second hexagon, rotating it as needed to reach each part. Allow the first hexagon to hang freely as you bead the second hexagon, to keep it out of the way. Make sure not to catch any part of the first hexagon as you bead the second hexagon. The two hexagons should be completely unconnected to each other, but linked together.

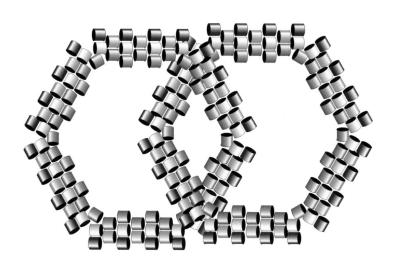

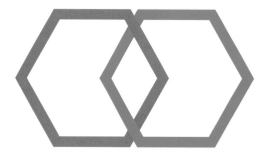

Of course, any shapes can be linked in this manner.

To entangle hexagons, construct a new hexagon linked through two hexagons where they join.

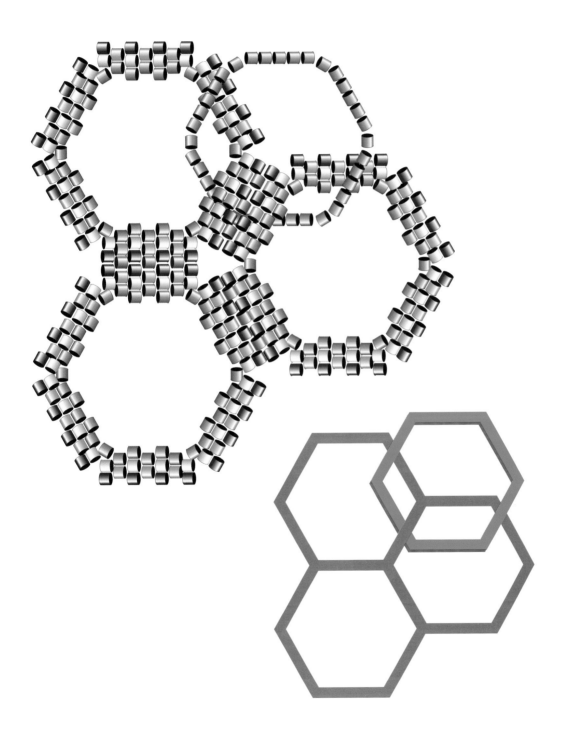

In the illustration below, three new hexagons are constructed, each entangled around one of the three joined sides. Those three new hexagons could be joined to each other to make two layers.

Pinching and Attaching Shapes

In some cases, a three-dimensional beaded object may be too flexible. Pinching and attaching sides to each other helps to stiffen the object and give it more definition. This is particularly useful when you are beading shapes with large Multiples. I've found that cubes look especially nice when their sides are pinched and attached.

Find a bead from Round One—the Foundation Ring—that is sticking down into the center of the shape, and is near the center. It doesn't have to be the exact center, just close to it. If an even number of beads sticks into the center, just use one that is next to the center.

In the illustration below, the bead you would use is indicated with a star.

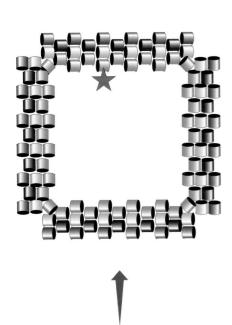

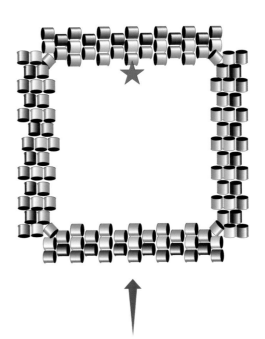

This square was beaded with a Multiple of five, and has four Round One beads sticking in toward the center on each side.

This square was beaded with a Multiple of six, and has five Round One beads sticking in toward the center on each side.

After two shapes are beaded and joined together, and the Spine is beaded, don't end your working thread yet. Fold and pinch the two shapes together with the Spine on the outside. This brings the Foundation Ring beads of each shape next to each other. Travel your needle down until it is coming out of the Foundation Ring bead that is near the center.

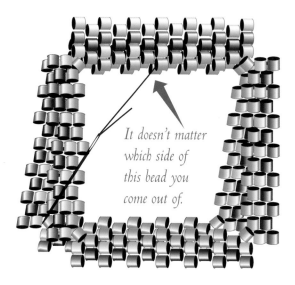

It doesn't matter which side of this bead you come out of.

Attach this Foundation Ring bead to the bead in the same position on the other shape, by looping through it several times.

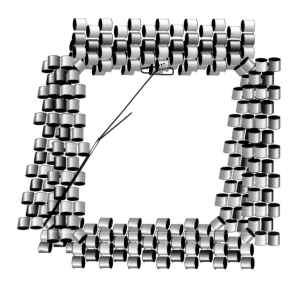

Every time you join two sides and bead a Spine, pinch the two sides together and attach two Foundation Ring beads near the center of each shape together. This has the effect of stiffening and defining the finished shape.

These two squares have been pinched and attached.

Here is an example of a cube that is not pinched and attached (left), and one that is (right). See the difference?

"Go away. Can't you tell I'm invisible?"

These thirteen projects represent just a small portion of the designs that can be made using these techniques. Please make sure you're familiar with the techniques in Part One before you begin. Each project uses one or more of the variations in Part Two, and refers back to those instructions. You might wish to become familiar with the relevant variations for your particular project before you begin.

Honeycomb Necklace

Star Sphere

Three Ivory Spheres

Rainbow Sphere

Stars and Stripes Forever

Octagon Sphere

Entangled Spheres

Mystery Weave Bracelet

Entangled Cubes Necklace

Seven Cubes Necklace

Pinched Cube Chain Necklace

Byzantine Chain Necklace

Chain Maille Necklace

Honeycomb Necklace

This necklace is made of 29 hexagons joined on edge, with no Spines added to the joins. The body of the necklace is about 4¾ inches wide by about 5 inches tall. Two shades of gold give it a subtle depth and the illusion of being in three dimensions.

THE MODEL

Shopping
    15 grams Aiko 712—Shiny Gold
    20 grams Aiko 712F—Matte Gold

Calculating the Foundation Ring
    Hexagons: 6 sides x 2 = a Base Number of 12.
                Each hexagon is made with a Multiple of 3.
                Base Number x Multiple = 36, so there are 36 beads
                in the Foundation Ring.
Techniques in Addition to Basics:
    Flat Odd-Count Peyote Stitch—see page 223

Beading the Hexagons

ROUND ONE
Use 36 beads of matte gold.

ROUND TWO
Bead this round entirely in shiny gold.

ROUND THREE
Bead this round entirely in shiny gold.

*Note: In these illustrations, the matte gold beads
are represented in yellow, and the shiny
gold beads are represented in red.*

Position each hexagon so there is a point at the top and bottom, and straight
vertical sides to the left and right.

Joining the Hexagons

Stitch the hexagons together using a single side of Round Four as if it were a Joining Row. Please see page 21 for specific details on joining shapes with three rounds. Use matte gold beads wherever you join two hexagons together.

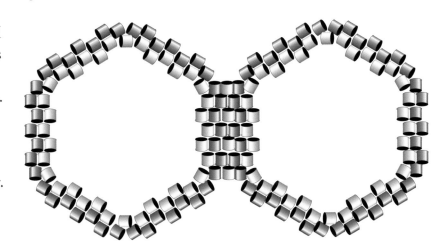

Continue beading and joining hexagons in horizontal rows. The bottom row has three hexagons, the second row has four hexagons, the third row has five hexagons, the fourth row has six hexagons, and the fifth row has five hexagons. Use matte gold beads wherever you join two hexagons together.

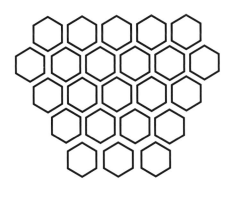

Attach three more hexagons onto each angled side of the outermost hexagons of the top row.

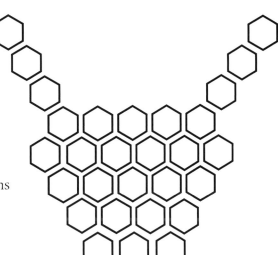

Beading the Strap

Bead two strips of peyote stitch, seven beads wide, for the strap, using the pattern to the right. Because this is odd-count flat peyote, you will have to do a "funny turn" at the end of every other row. (See page 223 for detailed directions on peyote stitch.) Bead this whatever length you prefer, but make both halves match. On the model, these straps were approximately 10 inches long each.

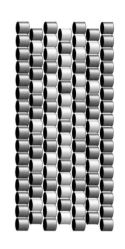

On one end of each strap, taper to three beads wide. Bead two rows of five beads wide, then two rows of three beads wide. Attach each tapered point to half of a clasp.

Loop the other end of each strap through a topmost hexagon and stitch it to itself.

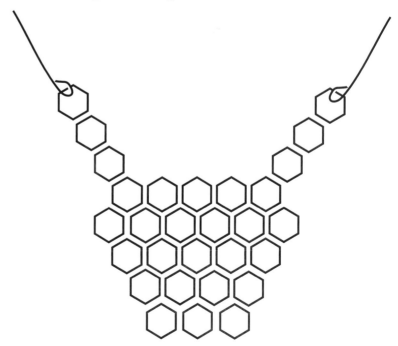

Star Sphere

This sphere is made of 20 hexagons and 12 pentagons, each with a Multiple of three. It is about 2½ inches in diameter.

THE MODELS

Shopping

Blue-Green Model:

    15 grams Aiko 710—Background Color: Blue-Green

    8 grams Aiko 712—Star Color: Gold

Purple Model:

    15 grams Aiko 704—Background Color: Purple

    8 grams Aiko 712—Star Color: Gold

Calculating the Foundation Ring

Pentagons: 5 sides x 2 = a Base Number of 10.

    Each pentagon is made with a Multiple of 3.

    Base Number x Multiple = 30, so there are 30 beads

    in the Foundation Ring of each pentagon.

Hexagons: 6 sides x 2 = a Base Number of 12.

    Each hexagon is made with a Multiple of 3.

    Base Number x Multiple = 36, so there are 36 beads

    in the Foundation Ring of each hexagon.

Techniques in Addition to Basics:

    Making Different Shapes *(pentagons)*—see page 24

    Turning Shapes into Stars—see page 39

    Sphere Assembly—see page 201

The First Shape—a Pentagon Star

ROUND ONE

Pick up 30 beads in the following pattern:

Two Star Color, one Background Color, two Star Color, one Background Color (etc.)

The last bead you pick up will be a Background Color, and there will be a total of ten Background Color beads.

Pass your needle through all 30 beads again,
and through a few more, to make a circle.
Have your needle come out after you have
passed through two Star Color beads—between
a Star Color and a Background Color, with the
Background Color bead next, right after the needle.

Leave a tail long enough to sew in later—
six or eight inches. You should be beading
with a firm, but not tight, tension.

*Note: In these illustrations, the Background Color
beads are represented in blue, and the Star Color
beads are represented in red.*

ROUND TWO

Pick up two Star Color beads,
skip the Background Color bead on the circle, and
stitch through one Star Color bead on the circle. The
two Star Color beads you have added sit on top of the
Background Color bead.

Pick up one Background Color bead, skip a bead
on the circle (Star Color), and stitch through the
next bead on the
circle (Background
Color). Pick up one
Background Color bead,
skip a bead on the circle
(Star Color), and stitch through the
next bead on the circle (Star Color).

*A Multiple of three means
there will be two single
stitches between corners.*

Notice that the two Background Color beads you have added form a "V" with a Background Color bead on the circle. Continue in this pattern all the way around the circle: add two Star Color beads, one Background Color bead, one Background Color bead. You will do this a total of five times to come around to the beginning of the circle.

At the end of this round, after you have added the last of the two individual Background Color beads, stitch through the first two Star Color beads you added in the beginning of this round. This steps up to the next round.

ROUND THREE

Using all Background Color beads, stitch around the circle, adding one bead at a time. When you come to the two Star Color beads, pass through them both without adding a bead between them.

At the end of this round, after you have added the last Background Color bead, pass your needle through both of the two Star Color beads.

Do not step up at the end of Round Three.

ROUND THREE-AND-A-HALF—
The Point of the Star

Pass your needle down through the next
three Star Color beads,
toward the center
of the circle.

Add one Star Color bead to complete the
"V" shape, the point of the star. Pass your
needle up through three Star Color beads.

Continue around the inside of the pentagon,
stitching through Star Color beads only, adding
a single bead of Star Color at the bottom of
each "V" to complete the points of the five-
sided star shape. After you have added the last
Star Color bead, pass your needle up through
all three Star Color beads in a line, to come out
between two Star Color beads.

ROUND FOUR

Bead Round Four, using all Background Color
beads, the same way as for all other shapes.
Please see page 9 for specific details on beading
Round Four.

The Second Shape—a Hexagon Star

Bead another shape—a six-sided hexagon star. Bead it the same way as the pentagon star, except pick up 36 beads for the Foundation Ring. Use the same pattern of beads for the Foundation Ring:

Two Star Color, one Background Color, two Star Color, one Background Color (etc.)

Please see page 39 for specific details on beading stars.

Join the hexagon star to the first shape—the pentagon star. Use Background Color beads for the Joining Row. Bead a Spine at the join using Background Color beads.

Please see pages 15–20 for specific details on joining shapes with four rounds and beading Spines. Detailed information on the method for assembling the entire sphere begins on page 201.

Three Ivory Spheres

Three Ivory Spheres looks very impressive, but it is surprisingly simple to make. It's about 4 inches in diameter.

Each of the three spheres is made of 20 hexagons and 12 pentagons. Each sphere has a different Multiple. The smallest sphere has a Multiple of two. The medium sphere has a Multiple of four. The largest sphere has a Multiple of six.

These directions are for the larger version of Three Ivory Spheres, shown on the left in the photograph below. The smaller version (on the right) is made with its smallest sphere having a Multiple of one, its medium sphere having a Multiple of three, and its largest sphere having a Multiple of five.

THE LARGER MODEL

Shopping

27 grams Aiko 764—Darkest Ivory

30 grams Aiko 763—Medium Ivory

38 grams Aiko 762—Lightest Ivory

Calculating the Foundation Rings

Pentagons: 5 sides x 2 = a Base Number of 10.

Small Sphere's Pentagon is made with a Multiple of 2. Base Number x Multiple = 20, so there are 20 beads in the Foundation Ring of each small pentagon.

Medium Sphere's Pentagon is made with a Multiple of 4. Base Number x Multiple = 40, so there are 40 beads in the Foundation Ring of each medium pentagon.

Large Sphere's Pentagon is made with a Multiple of 6. Base Number x Multiple = 60, so there are 60 beads in the Foundation Ring of each large pentagon.

Hexagons: 6 sides x 2 = a Base Number of 12.

Small Sphere's Hexagon is made with a Multiple of 2. Base Number x Multiple = 24, so there are 24 beads in the Foundation Ring of each small hexagon.

Medium Sphere's Hexagon is made with a Multiple of 4. Base Number x Multiple = 48, so there are 48 beads in the Foundation Ring of each medium hexagon.

Large Sphere's Hexagon is made with a Multiple of 6. Base Number x Multiple = 72, so there are 72 beads in the Foundation Ring of each large hexagon.

Techniques in Addition to Basics:

Making Different Shapes *(pentagons)*—see page 24

Making Different Sizes—see page 27

Sphere Assembly—see page 201

We're going to bead half a sphere at a time, then join the two halves together. We'll bead the small sphere first, and join its two halves together. Then we'll bead the two halves of the medium sphere, put the completed small sphere inside, and join the two halves of the medium sphere together. Then we'll bead the two halves of the large sphere, put the medium sphere (which already contains the small sphere) inside, and join the two halves of the large sphere together.

The First Shape—the Small Sphere's Pentagon

ROUND ONE

All the shapes in the small sphere use a Multiple of two. Pick up 20 beads for the Foundation Ring. Use the Darkest Ivory color for Round One.

Pass your needle through all 20 beads again, to make a circle. Continue on through a few more beads (it doesn't matter how many) so that your needle is coming out of a different place than your tail.

Leave a tail long enough to sew in later—six or eight inches. You should be beading with a firm, but not tight, tension.

Note: These colors are so subtle and closely related to each other that illustrations using them would not be clear. In the illustrations that follow, the Round One beads are represented in red.

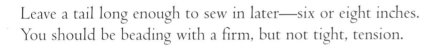

ROUND TWO

Use the Medium Ivory color for Round Two.

Pick up two beads, skip one bead on the Foundation Ring, and stitch through the next bead in the circle.

Note: In these illustrations, the Round Two beads are represented in yellow.

Pick up one bead, skip one bead on the Foundation Ring, and stitch through the next bead in the circle.

Continue beading around the Foundation Ring in this pattern, adding two beads, then one bead, then two beads, until you come around to the beginning. The pairs of beads form the corners of the pentagon.

At the end of this round, after you have added the last single bead, stitch through the first two beads you added in the beginning of this round. This steps up to the next round.

A Multiple of two means there will be one single stitch between corners.

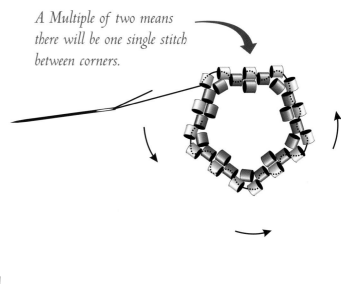

ROUND THREE
Use the Medium Ivory color for Round Three.

Stitch around the pentagon, adding one bead at a time. When you come to the pairs of beads that form the corners, pass through them both without adding a bead between them.

At the end of this round, after you have added the last bead, pass your needle through one of the pair of beads. Your needle will come out between the two beads of the pair that forms a corner. Do not step up at the end of Round Three.

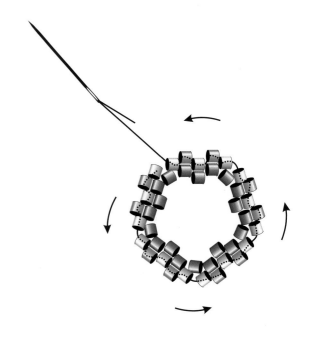

Note: In these illustrations, the Round Three beads are represented in green.

ROUND FOUR

Bead Round Four, using the Lightest Ivory color, as detailed on page 9.

Note: In these illustrations, the Round Four beads are represented in blue.

A Multiple of two means there will be three beads on each finished side in Round Four.

The Second Shape—a Hexagon

Bead another shape—a six-sided hexagon. Bead it the same way as the pentagon, except pick up 24 beads for the Foundation Ring. Use the same colors—Darkest Ivory for Round One, Medium Ivory for Round Two and Round Three, and Lightest Ivory for Round Four.

Join the hexagon to the first shape, the pentagon, using Lightest Ivory beads for the Joining Row. Bead a Spine at the join using Lightest Ivory beads.

Please see pages 15–20 for more detailed information on joining shapes and beading Spines.

Note: In these illustrations, the Joining Row beads are represented in purple. For clarity, the Spines are not shown.

Detailed information on the method for assembling the entire sphere begins on page 201.

The Medium Sphere

Using the same method as the small sphere, bead pentagons and hexagons for the medium sphere, using a Multiple of four.

The pentagons in the medium sphere will use 40 beads in the Foundation Ring, and the hexagons will use 48 beads in the Foundation Ring.

Use the same colors as the small sphere: Darkest Ivory for Round One, Medium Ivory for Round Two and Round Three, and Lightest Ivory for Round Four. Use Lightest Ivory for the Joining Rows and the Spines.

A Multiple of four means there will be three single stitches between corners in Round Two.

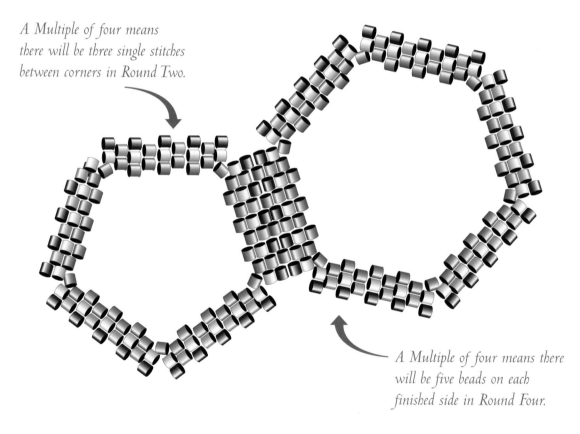

A Multiple of four means there will be five beads on each finished side in Round Four.

Bead two complete halves of the medium sphere. Detailed information on the method for assembling the entire sphere begins on page 201. Place the completed small sphere inside the two halves as you join them. You may find it easier to join about a third of the way around the two medium halves, then insert the small sphere. Make sure you don't go too far in joining before inserting it!

The Large Sphere

Using the same method as the small sphere and the medium sphere, bead pentagons and hexagons for the large sphere, using a Multiple of six.

The pentagons in the large sphere will use 60 beads in the Foundation Ring, and the hexagons will use 72 beads in the Foundation Ring.

Use the same colors as the other two spheres: Darkest Ivory for Round One, Medium Ivory for Round Two and Round Three, and Lightest Ivory for Round Four. Use Lightest Ivory for the Joining Rows and the Spines.

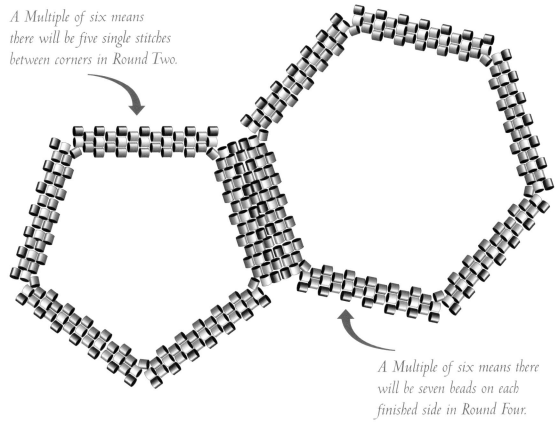

A Multiple of six means there will be five single stitches between corners in Round Two.

A Multiple of six means there will be seven beads on each finished side in Round Four.

Bead two complete halves of the large sphere. Detailed information on the method for assembling the entire sphere begins on page 201. Place the completed medium sphere, which already contains the completed small sphere, inside the two halves as you join them. You may find it easier to join about a third of the way around the two large halves, then insert the medium sphere. Make sure you don't go too far in joining before inserting it!

When I first had the idea that led to the Three Ivory Spheres, I planned to make the project with six nested spheres. I was inspired by Chinese carved ivory puzzle balls, which have many freely rotating layers carved from a single chunk of ivory. The smallest beaded sphere would have a Multiple of one, the next larger sphere would have a Multiple of two, and so on. I beaded all twelve halves of the six spheres, checking to make sure they fit inside each other as I worked. At last, I joined the two halves of the smallest sphere with the Multiple of one, and then started to join the next sphere over it. To my chagrin, I thought it looked terrible. The layers were too close together, and you couldn't see through the spheres. An experiment where I put all six spheres together temporarily looked even worse— it was a big, visually confusing mess.

You can imagine how I felt at this point—that's a lot of beading to have a project fail! To make things worse, I had worked on this on and off for almost a year, and had planned the project as an entry in the 2006 Treasures of Toho contest. The deadline was getting pretty close, and I was so upset I was ready to forget the contest entirely. A great deal of bad language was used!

I have to give my husband Richard complete credit for saving the day with his brilliantly simple idea. He suggested I use every other sphere and make three layers. This spaced out the layers enough so they were much more visually pleasing. I used the spheres with the Multiples of two, four, and six. Three Ivory Spheres was completed in time for the contest, and I was greatly honored to be the winner in the All Aiko category. As a bonus, I also had a second version of Three Ivory Spheres, using the spheres with the Multiples of one, three, and five. Fortunately the contest prize was a trip to Japan for two, because without Richard there would never have been an entry at all!

Miyajima Island was one of the highlights of our trip to Japan.

Rainbow Sphere

The Rainbow Sphere is constructed with filled hexagons and open pentagon stars. Bright colors emphasize the geometric nature of the sphere. It's about 2½ inches in diameter. There are 12 pentagon stars and 20 filled hexagons. The pentagon stars use a Multiple of three, and the filled hexagons are a corresponding size.

THE MODEL

Shopping

11 grams Aiko 45A—Red
7 grams Aiko 50—Orange
10 grams Aiko 42—Yellow
4 grams Aiko 47—Green
7 grams Aiko 43—Blue

Calculating the Foundation Ring

Pentagons: 5 sides x 2 = a Base Number of 10.

The pentagon star is made with a Multiple of 3.
Base Number x Multiple = 30, so there are 30 beads
in the Foundation Ring of each pentagon star.

Hexagons: Shapes with a Multiple of three will have four beads on each
side when Round Four is completed. The filled hexagons will
also have four beads on each side when finished, so they can be
joined to the pentagon stars.

Techniques in Addition to Basics:

Making Different Shapes (*pentagons*)—see page 24
Turning Shapes into Stars—see page 39
Filled Shapes—see page 31
Sphere Assembly—see page 201

We're going to bead half the sphere at a time, then join the two halves together.

The First Shape—a Pentagon Star

ROUND ONE

Pick up 30 beads in
the following pattern:

> Two Yellow, one Green,
> two Yellow, one Green (etc.)

The last bead you pick up will be
Green, and there will be a total of
ten Green beads.

Pass your needle through all 30
beads again, and through a few
more, to make a circle. Have your
needle come out after you have
passed through two Yellow beads—
between a Yellow and a Green,
with the Green bead next, right
after the needle.

Leave a tail long enough to sew in later—
six or eight inches. You should
be beading with a firm, but not
tight, tension.

ROUND TWO

Pick up two Yellow beads, skip the
Green bead on the circle, and stitch
through one Yellow bead on the
circle. The two Yellow beads you have
added sit on top of the Green bead.

Pick up one Green bead, skip a bead on the circle (Yellow), and stitch through the next bead on the circle (Green). Pick up one Green bead, skip a bead on the circle (Yellow), and stitch through the next bead on the circle (Yellow).

A Multiple of three means there will be two single stitches between corners.

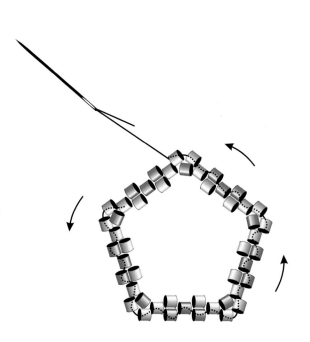

Notice that the two Green beads you have added form a "V" with a Green bead on the circle. Continue in this pattern all the way around the circle: add two Yellow beads, one Green bead, one Green bead. You will do this a total of five times to come around to the beginning of the circle.

At the end of this round, after you have added the last of the two individual Green beads, stitch through the first two Yellow beads you added in the beginning of this round. This steps up to the next round.

ROUND THREE

Using all Green beads, stitch around
the circle, adding one bead at a time.
When you come to the two Yellow beads,
pass through them both without adding a
bead between them.

At the end of this round, after you have
added the last Green bead, pass your needle
through both of the two Yellow beads.

Do not step up at the end of Round Three.

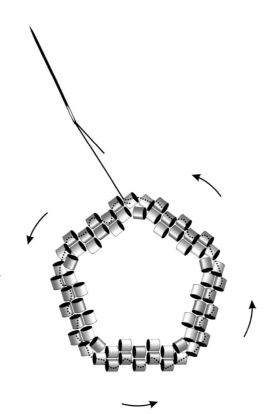

ROUND THREE-AND-A-HALF—The Point of the Star

Pass your needle down through
the next three Yellow beads, toward
the center of the circle.

Add one Yellow bead
to complete the "V"
shape, the point of
the star. Pass your needle up
through three Yellow beads.

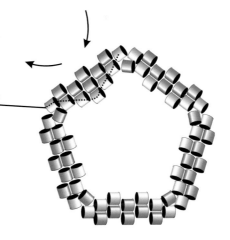

Continue around the inside of the pentagon, stitching through Yellow beads only, adding a single Yellow bead at the bottom of each "V" to complete the points of the five-sided star shape. After you have added the last Yellow bead, pass your needle up through all three Yellow beads in a line, to come out between two Yellow beads.

ROUND FOUR
Bead Round Four, using Blue beads, as detailed on page 9.

The Second Shape—a Filled Hexagon

Bead another shape—a six-sided filled hexagon, which will be the same size as if we had used a Multiple of three for an open hexagon. The finished filled hexagon will have four beads on each side, and can be joined to the pentagon star constructed with a Multiple of three. Please see page 31 for detailed information on beading filled shapes. The example on those pages is a hexagon of the same size as you will be beading, so you can follow the steps exactly, changing the colors as needed.

ROUND ONE

Make a circle of six Yellow beads.
Pass your needle through all six
beads again, and through a few
more, so your needle is coming out
of a different place than your tail.

ROUND TWO

Add one Yellow bead in between
each Yellow bead from Round One.
After adding the last bead in
Round Two, step up by stitching
through one more bead—the first
bead that was added.

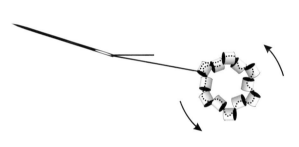

ROUND THREE

Add two Yellow beads between each sticking-up bead
from Round Two. At the end of this round, step up
by going through the first two beads you added.

ROUNDS FOUR THROUGH ELEVEN

Continue beading the filled hexagon as detailed on page 31. The colors for the rounds are as follows:

Round Four—all Yellow.
Round Five—all Yellow.
Round Six—the single bead on top of the Yellow beads is Yellow; the pair
　　　　　of beads added together over the wide gap is Orange.
Round Seven—all Orange.
Round Eight—all Orange.
Round Nine—all Red.
Round Ten—all Red.
Round Eleven—all Red.

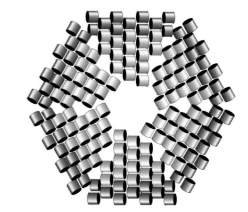

Constructing the Sphere

We're going to bead half the sphere
at a time, then join the two halves together.

Join the filled hexagon to the first shape, the pentagon star, using Blue beads for the Joining Row. Bead a Spine at the join using Blue beads.

Please see pages 15–20 for more detailed
information on joining shapes and beading Spines.
Detailed information on the method for assembling
the entire sphere begins on page 201.

Wherever a filled hexagon is joined to a pentagon
star, use Blue beads for the Joining Row and
the Spine. Wherever a filled hexagon is
joined to another filled hexagon,
use Red beads for the Joining Row
and the Spine.

*Note: For clarity, the Spines are not shown
in the illustration to the right.*

Stars and Stripes Forever

Stars and Stripes Forever is a sphere that differs from Star Sphere and Rainbow Sphere by being constructed using only twelve large pentagon stars. It's about 2 inches in diameter. The pentagon stars are beaded with a Multiple of five.

THE MODEL

Shopping
    4 grams Aiko 45A—Red
    8 grams Aiko 41—White
    6 grams Aiko 48—Blue

Calculating the Foundation Ring
    Pentagon Stars: 5 sides x 2 = a Base Number of 10.
              The pentagon star is made with a Multiple of 5.
              Base Number x Multiple = 50, so there are 50 beads
              in the Foundation Ring of each pentagon star.

Techniques in Addition to Basics:
    Making Different Shapes *(pentagons)*—see page 24
    Turning Shapes into Stars—see page 39

We're going to bead half the sphere at a time, then join the two halves together.

The Pentagon Star

ROUND ONE
Pick up 50 beads in
the following pattern:

    Two Blue, one Red, two Blue,
    two White, one Red, two White
    (etc.)

Pass your needle through all 50
beads again, and through a few more,
to make a circle. Have your needle come
out after you have passed through two White
beads—between a White bead and a Red bead,
with the Red bead next, right after the needle.

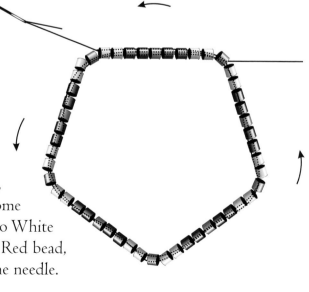

Leave a tail long enough to sew in later—six or eight inches. You should be beading with a firm, but not tight, tension.

ROUND TWO
Pick up two White beads, skip the Red bead on the circle, and stitch through one White bead on the circle. The two White beads you have added sit on top of the Red bead.

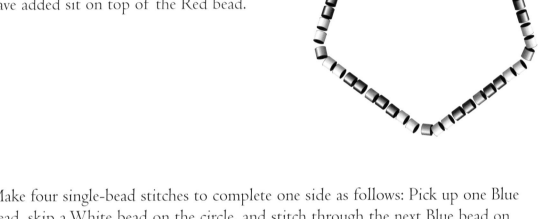

Make four single-bead stitches to complete one side as follows: Pick up one Blue bead, skip a White bead on the circle, and stitch through the next Blue bead on the circle. Pick up one White bead, skip a Blue bead on the circle, and stitch through the next Red bead on the circle. Pick up one White bead, skip a Blue bead on the circle, and stitch through the next Blue bead on the circle. Pick up one Blue bead, skip a White bead on the circle, and stitch through the next White bead on the circle.

A Multiple of five means there will be four single-bead stitches between corners in Round Two.

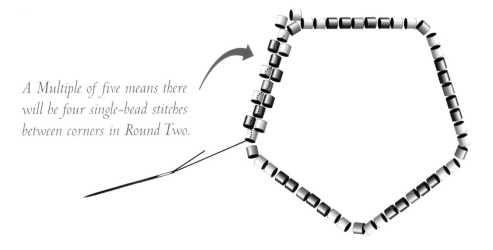

104

Continue beading the
remaining four sides
of the pentagon star in the
same pattern: two White beads on top of a
Red bead, then one Blue bead, one White
bead, one White bead, and one Blue bead.

At the end of this round, after you have
added the last Blue bead, stitch through
the first two White beads you added in the
beginning of this round. This steps up to
the next round.

ROUND THREE

Using the following color pattern, stitch around the pentagon, adding one bead at
a time. When you come to the two White beads, pass through them both without
adding a bead between them.

Immediately after stitching
through two White beads, add
one Blue bead, one Red bead, one
Red bead, one Red bead, and one
Blue bead. Repeat all the way around
the pentagon.

At the end of this round, after you have
added the last Blue bead, pass your needle
through both of the two White beads.

Do not step up at the end
of Round Three.

ROUND THREE-AND-A-HALF—
The Point of the Star

Stitch down through two White beads, toward the center of the pentagon star. Make three single stitches: one White bead, one Blue bead, one White bead. Stitch back up through three White beads to come out between the two White beads that form the corner.

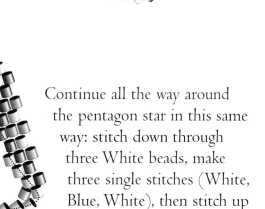

Continue all the way around the pentagon star in this same way: stitch down through three White beads, make three single stitches (White, Blue, White), then stitch up through three White beads.

Stitch all the way around the pentagon star again in the same manner. Stitch down through four White beads, add two stitches of one White bead each, and stitch up through four White beads, all the way around.

Stitch all the way around the pentagon star again in the same manner. This time, stitch down through five White beads, add one White bead to finish the point of the star, and stitch up through five White beads, all the way around.

After you have added the last White bead, stitch up through all five White beads in a line, to come out between two White beads.

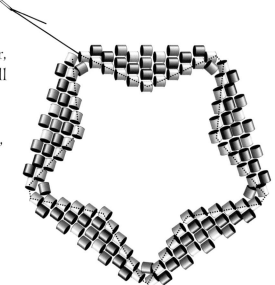

ROUND FOUR
Bead Round Four as detailed on page 9. Use the following color pattern. In Round Four, there are a total of six beads on each finished side of the pentagon star. The first bead is Blue, followed by four individual White beads, and the last bead is Blue.

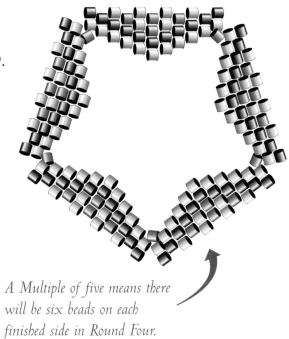

A Multiple of five means there will be six beads on each finished side in Round Four.

Constructing the Sphere

We're going to bead half the Stars and Stripes Forever sphere at a time, then join the two halves together. Bead another pentagon star exactly the same as the first one.

Join the second pentagon star to the first pentagon star. Use Red beads for the Joining Row. Bead a Spine at the join, and use the same color bead for the Spine as is already used on the beads underneath. (This continues the red and white stripes.)

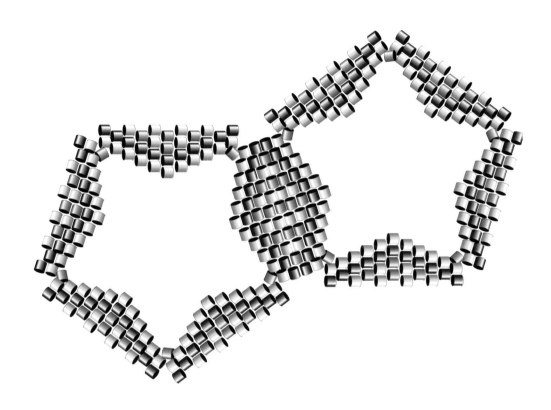

For the first row of the Spine, the bead colors are Blue, White, White, White, White, Blue. For the second row of the Spine, all five beads are Red.

Please see pages 15–20 for specific details on joining shapes and beading Spines.

Make another identical pentagon star and join it to the next side of the pentagon star. Use the same method as you used before, including making a Spine.

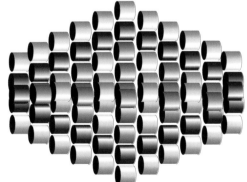

After you join the third pentagon star to the first pentagon star, travel your needle to the correct position and join the two adjacent sides of the second and third pentagon stars. Every time you join shapes together, bead a Spine on top of the join. Make sure the Spines are all on the outside of the sphere.

Join the third pentagon to the second pentagon.

Also join the third pentagon to the next side of the first pentagon.

Bead three more identical pentagon stars, and join one to each remaining side of the first pentagon star. Join each one to the adjacent side of the previous pentagon star as well. The fifth pentagon star will need to be joined on three sides.

You now have a ring of five pentagon stars around a single pentagon star. The ring forms a little dome. Think of the first pentagon star as the North Pole of the half-sphere you are beading.

This completes half the sphere. Now you get to go back and do it all again for the other half!

Once the two halves of the sphere are beaded, you will see that they fit together like two puzzle pieces. The protruding points of the pentagon stars of one half fit into the recessed "V" shapes between two pentagon stars of the other half.

To join the two halves into a sphere, align the halves into the proper orientation, and begin joining sides. Use the same method as you have been using all along, and join each side together around the equator of the sphere. Remember to bead a Spine every time you join two sides together. It may help to stuff a piece of fabric inside the two halves to give them some structure as you begin to join them, but don't forget to take it out before you go too far!

Octagon Sphere

The Octagon Sphere differs from Star Sphere and Rainbow Sphere by being constructed using eight-sided octagons, six-sided hexagons, and four-sided squares. All three shapes use a Multiple of five. There are six octagons, eight hexagons, and twelve squares in this sphere. The Octagon Sphere is about 4 inches in diameter.

THE MODEL

Shopping

    9 grams Aiko 36—Green
    10 grams Aiko 27BD—Aqua
    8 grams Aiko 28—Blue
    6 grams Aiko 712—Gold

Calculating the Foundation Rings

    All shapes use a Multiple of five.

Squares: 4 sides x 2 = a Base Number of 8.
Base Number x Multiple = 40, so there are 40 beads
in the Foundation Ring of each square.

Hexagons: 6 sides x 2 = a Base Number of 12.
Base Number x Multiple = 60, so there are 60 beads
in the Foundation Ring of each hexagon.

Octagons: 8 sides x 2 = a Base Number of 16.
Base Number x Multiple = 80.
Obtuse Angle Adjustment: Add one bead at each corner to
compensate for the obtuse angles of the octagon. Total of 8
beads added to the Foundation Ring of 80 = a total
compensated Foundation Ring of 88 beads.

Techniques in Addition to Basics:

    Making Different Shapes *(octagons, squares)*—see page 24
    Extremely Obtuse Angles—see page 51
    Pinching and Attaching Shapes—see page 69

We're going to bead half the sphere at a time, then join the halves together.

The First Shape—an Octagon

ROUND ONE

Pick up 88 Green beads for the Foundation Ring.

Pass your needle through all 88 beads again, and through a few more, to make a circle.

Leave a tail long enough to sew in later—six or eight inches. You should be beading with a firm, but not tight, tension.

ROUND TWO

Pick up three Aqua beads, skip the two Green beads on the circle, and stitch through one Green bead on the circle. This is part of the process of compensating the corners of a shape for extremely obtuse angles. See page 51 for specific information on this technique.

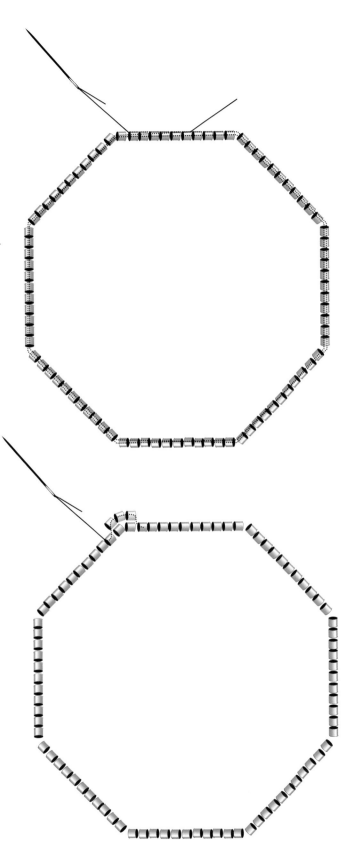

Make four single stitches of Aqua beads
to complete
one side of
the octagon.

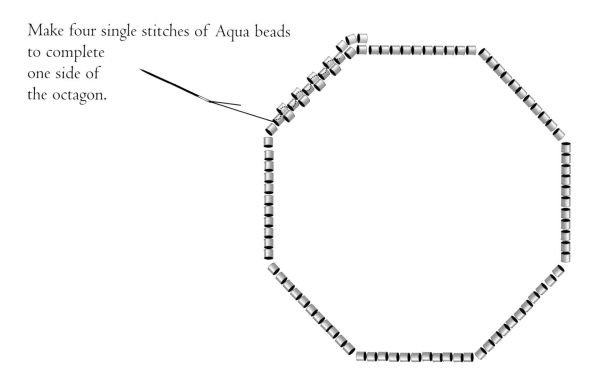

Bead this pattern all the way around the octagon: pick up three Aqua beads
and skip two Green beads
on the circle, make four
single stitches of Aqua
beads, pick up three Aqua beads
and skip two Green beads on the
circle, etc.

You will do this a total of eight
times to come around to the
beginning of the circle.

At the end of this round, after
you have added the last of the
four individual Aqua beads,
stitch through the first three
Aqua beads you added in the
beginning of this round. This
steps up to the next round.

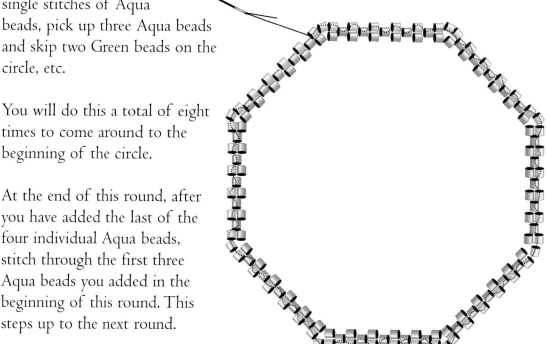

ROUND THREE

Using all Aqua beads, stitch around the circle, adding one bead at a time. When you come to the three Aqua beads from Round Two, pass through all three of them without adding a bead between them, **except at the end of the round.**

At the end of this round, after you have added the last single bead, pass your needle through the first Aqua bead of the three beads that were added in Round Two. Your needle will come out between the first and second beads of the three that form a corner. Do not step up at the end of Round Three.

ROUND FOUR

Bead Round Four, using Blue beads, as detailed on page 9. Ignore the center bead of the group of three Aqua beads that formed the corners in Round Two. Use the first and last bead of the group of three to build the Round Four sides.

A Multiple of five means there will be six beads on each finished side in Round Four.

The Second Shape—a Hexagon

Bead a hexagon using a Multiple of five. Use the same colors that were used in the octagon: Green for the Foundation Ring, Aqua for Round Two, Aqua for Round Three, and Blue for Round Four. Do not use the method of compensating corners for the hexagon.

ROUND ONE
Pick up 60 Green beads.

Pass your needle through all 60 beads again, and through a few more, to make a circle.

Leave a tail long enough to sew in later—six or eight inches. You should be beading with a firm, but not tight, tension.

ROUND TWO
Pick up two Aqua beads, skip one Green bead on the Foundation Ring, and stitch through the next bead in the circle. This is a normal, non-compensated corner.

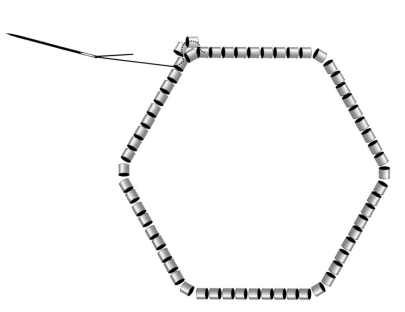

Make four more single stitches
of one Aqua bead each.

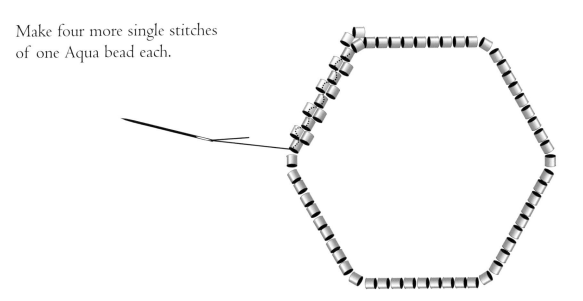

Bead this pattern all the way around the hexagon: pick up two Aqua beads and
skip a Green bead on the circle, make four single stitches of Aqua beads, pick up
two Aqua beads and skip a Green bead on the circle, etc.

You will do this
a total of six times
to come around to
the beginning of
the circle.

At the end of this
round, after you have
added the last of the four
individual Aqua beads, stitch
through the first two Aqua
beads you added in the beginning
of this round. This steps up to the
next round.

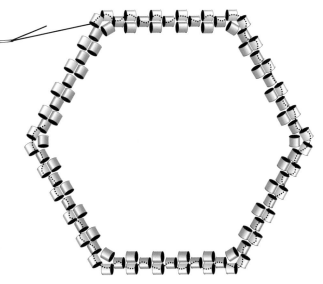

ROUND THREE

Stitch around the hexagon, adding one Aqua bead at a time. When you come to the pairs of beads that form the corners, pass through them both without adding a bead between them.

At the end of this round, after you have added the last bead, pass your needle through one of the pair of Aqua beads that formed the corner in Round Two. Your needle will come out between the two beads. Do not step up at the end of Round Three.

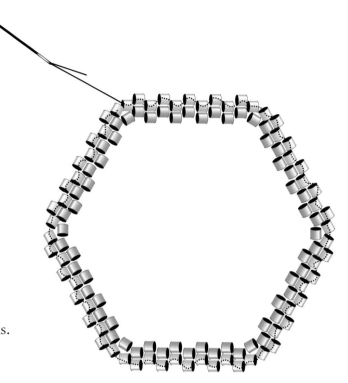

ROUND FOUR

Bead Round Four, using Blue beads, as detailed on page 9. Because we used a Multiple of five, there will be six beads on each finished side.

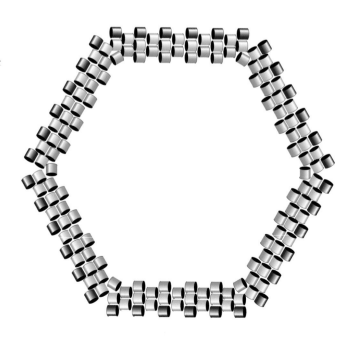

Joining the First Two Shapes

Join the hexagon to the octagon, using Blue beads. Bead a Spine using Gold beads. Pinch the two shapes and attach the one bead at the center of each shape's Foundation Ring (Green) together.

Please see pages 15–20 for more detailed information on joining shapes and beading Spines. Please see page 69 for more detailed information on pinching and attaching shapes.

Note: In this illustration, the Spine is not shown, and the two shapes have not yet been pinched and attached.

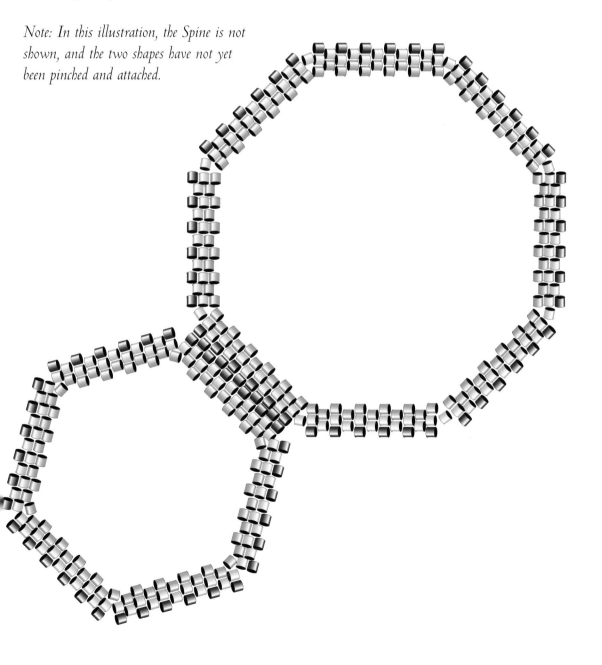

The Third Shape—a Square

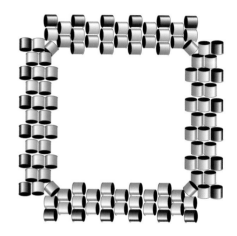

Bead a square using a Multiple of five, with 40 beads in the Foundation Ring. Use the same colors used in the octagon and hexagon: Green for the Foundation Ring, Aqua for Round Two, Aqua for Round Three, and Blue for Round Four. Do not use the method of compensating corners for the square.

Join the square to the side of the octagon next to the hexagon. After you have joined the square to the octagon, travel your needle to the next side and join the square to the hexagon.

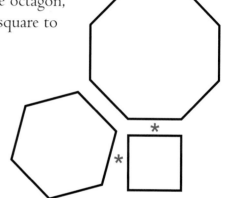

Every time you join two shapes, remember to bead a Spine using Gold beads. Pinch the two shapes and attach the one bead at the center of each shape's Foundation Ring (Green) together. Make sure the Spines are all on the outside of the sphere.

Constructing Half the Sphere

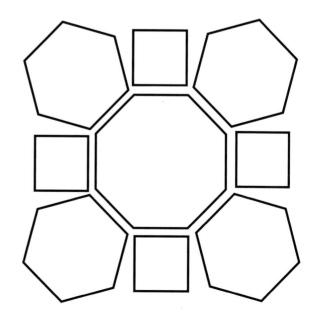

We're going to bead half the sphere at a time, then join the two halves together.

Bead a ring of alternating hexagons and squares around the outside of the first octagon.

Bead another octagon and two more squares. Attach the octagon to one side
of a square, opposite from the first octagon. Attach a square to each side of the
second octagon. Join as shown.

Every time you join two shapes, remember to bead a Spine using Gold beads.
Pinch the two shapes and attach the one bead at the center of each shape's
Foundation Ring (Green) together. Make sure the Spines are all on the outside
of the sphere.

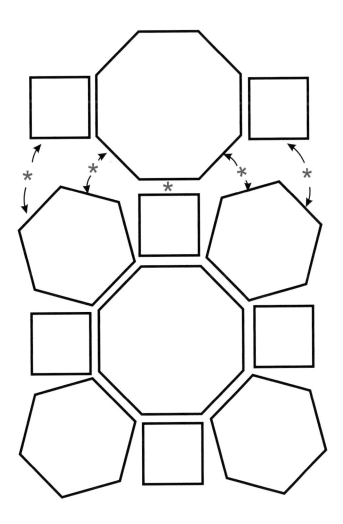

Bead one more octagon and attach it to one of the squares next to where the second octagon was attached.

Every time you join two shapes, remember to bead a Spine using Gold beads. Pinch the two shapes and attach the one bead at the center of each shape's Foundation Ring (Green) together. Make sure the Spines are all on the outside of the sphere.

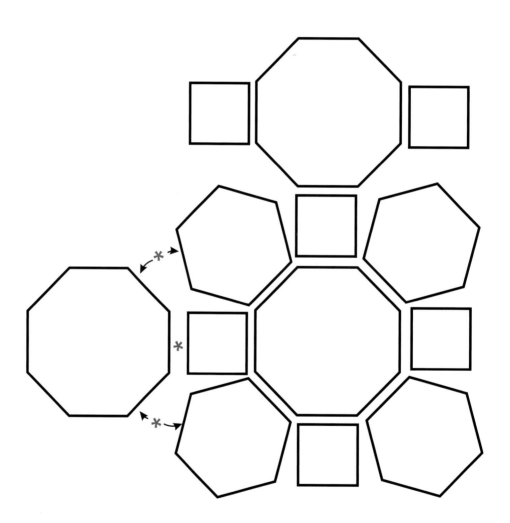

This completes the first half of the sphere. Now you get to go back and do it all again!

There is one difference between the two halves: they are mirror images of each other. When you attach the last octagon, you have to attach it to the **other** side. On the first half of the sphere, the last octagon was attached at the nine o'clock position. On the second half of the sphere, illustrated below, the last octagon is attached at the three o'clock position.

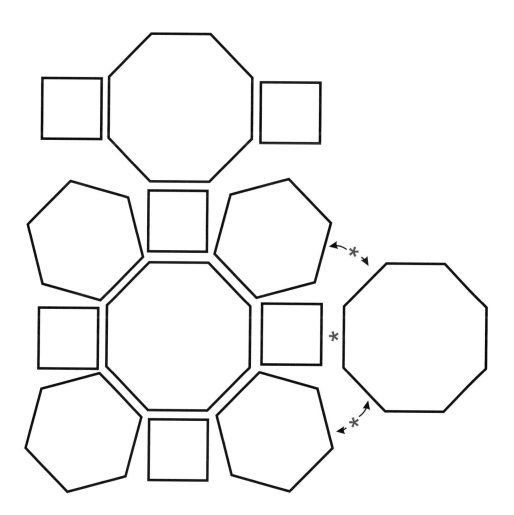

Compare the second half with the first half to see how they will fit together. Every octagon will be surrounded by a ring of alternating hexagons and squares. Join the two halves, one side at a time, traveling your needle to get into position to join the next side.

Every time you join two shapes, remember to bead a Spine using Gold beads. Pinch the two shapes and attach the one bead at the center of each shape's Foundation Ring (Green) together. Make sure the Spines are all on the outside of the sphere.

Judy and her two helpers

Entangled Spheres

The two spheres that make up the Entangled Spheres are woven through each other as if one is passing through the other. The colors are the reverse of each other—one is a black sphere with gold accents, and the other is a gold sphere with black accents. Each sphere is made of 20 hexagons and 12 pentagons, with a Multiple of three. Each sphere is about 3 inches in diameter, and the two spheres together are about 6 inches wide.

This is a challenging project and I recommend that this not be the first sphere you attempt!

THE MODEL

Shopping
    40 grams Delica size 10/0, color number 10—Black
    40 grams Delica size 10/0, color number 31—Gold

I found that Entangled Spheres made with the new size 10/0 Delicas were more flexible than spheres made with standard-sized Delicas or Aikos. I used Nymo size D, and I think that heavier thread might have fixed this. If you are using regular cylinder beads, such as standard-sized Delicas or Aikos, you would need about 25 grams of each color.

Calculating the Foundation Rings
    Pentagons: 5 sides x 2 = a Base Number of 10.
            The pentagon is made with a Multiple of 3.
            Base Number x Multiple = 30, so there are 30 beads
            in the Foundation Ring of each pentagon.

    Hexagons: 6 sides x 2 = a Base Number of 12.
            The hexagon is made with a Multiple of 3.
            Base Number x Multiple = 36, so there are 36 beads
            in the Foundation Ring of each hexagon.

Techniques in Addition to Basics:
    Making Different Shapes *(pentagons)*—see page 24
    Linking and Entangling Shapes—see page 65
    Sphere Assembly—see page 201

We're going to bead a small part of the first (Black) sphere, then bead the corresponding part of the second (Gold) sphere entangled through the first part. Then we're going to add the remaining shapes to make each small part into half a sphere. We'll bead another half-sphere for each side and join them to make complete spheres.

The First Shape—a Black Pentagon

ROUND ONE

Pick up 30 beads for the Foundation Ring in the following pattern:

Five Black, one Gold, five Black, one Gold (etc.)

Pass your needle through all 30 beads again, to make a circle. Continue on through a few more beads so that your needle comes out after the five Black beads, between a Black bead and a Gold bead. The Gold bead should be next, right after the needle.

Leave a tail long enough to sew in later— six or eight inches. You should be beading with a firm, but not tight, tension.

ROUND TWO

Pick up two Gold beads, skip the Gold bead on the circle, and stitch through one Black bead on the circle.
The two Gold beads you have added sit on top of the Gold bead on the circle.

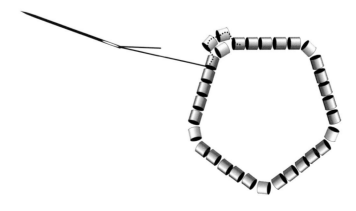

Pick up one Black bead, skip a bead on the circle (Black), and stitch through the next bead on the circle (Black). Pick up one Black bead, skip a bead on the circle (Black), and stitch through the next bead on the circle (Black).

A Multiple of three means there will be two single stitches between corners.

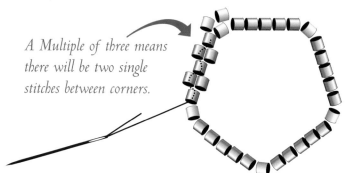

Continue beading around the Foundation Ring in this pattern, adding two Gold beads, then two single stitches of one Black bead each, then two Gold beads, until you come around to the beginning. The pairs of Gold beads form the corners of the pentagon. Each pair of Gold beads sits on top of a Gold bead from the Foundation Ring.

At the end of this round, after you have added the last single Black bead, stitch through the first two Gold beads you added in the beginning of this round. This steps up to the next round.

ROUND THREE
Using all Black beads, stitch around the circle, adding one bead at a time. When you come to the two Gold beads, pass through them both without adding a bead between them.

At the end of this round, after you have added the last Black bead, pass your needle through one of the two Gold beads, coming out between them.

Do not step up at the end of Round Three.

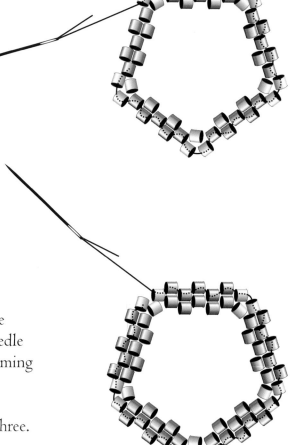

ROUND FOUR

Bead Round Four as detailed on page 9. Use the following color pattern. The first bead of each side of Round Four will be Gold, then a Black bead, a Black bead, then a Gold bead. Notice that each corner has a little "V" of Gold beads.

The Second Shape—a Black Hexagon

Bead another shape—a six-sided hexagon. Bead it the same way as the pentagon, except pick up 36 beads for the Foundation Ring. Use the same pattern to pick up the Foundation Ring—five Black, one Gold, five Black, one Gold (etc.).

Join the hexagon to the first shape (the pentagon) using Black beads for the Joining Row. Bead a Spine at the join using Gold beads on top of Gold, Black beads on top of Black. When you bead the Spine, the first and last beads of the first row are Gold, with two Black beads in between. The second row of the Spine are all Black beads.

Please see pages 15–20 for more detailed information on joining shapes and beading Spines.

Make another hexagon, and join it to the next side of the pentagon. Use the same method as you used before, including making a Spine.

Join the second hexagon to the next side of the pentagon.

After you join the second hexagon to the pentagon, travel your needle to the correct position and join the two adjacent sides of the two hexagons. Every time you join shapes together, bead a Spine on top of the join. Make sure all the Spines are on the same side—the outside of the sphere.

Also join the second hexagon to the first hexagon.

Bead three more hexagons, and join one to each remaining side of the pentagon. Join each one to the adjacent side of the previous hexagon as well. The fifth hexagon will need to be joined on three sides.

You now have a ring of five hexagons around a single pentagon. The ring forms a little dome. Remember to think of the first pentagon as the North Pole of the half-sphere you are beading. This completes the first small part of the first (Black) sphere.

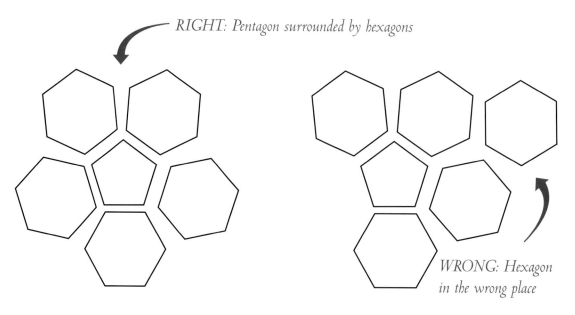

RIGHT: Pentagon surrounded by hexagons

WRONG: Hexagon in the wrong place

Be careful where you attach each hexagon—it's easy to get mixed up and attach it between two hexagons, instead of attaching it to a side of the pentagon.

Constructing the Second Sphere

Now we will bead the same small part of
the second (Gold) sphere. Each Gold
hexagon will be entangled through two
hexagons of the small part of the Black
sphere you have already beaded.

Bead a pentagon with a Foundation Ring
of 30 beads like the one you did before,
but with reversed colors. Pick up a pattern
of five Gold, one Black, five Gold,
one Black (etc.) for the Foundation Ring.

Start the first Gold hexagon of the ring of five hexagons that goes around the first
Gold pentagon. Pick up 36 beads for the Foundation Ring in the same pattern as
the pentagon: five Gold, one Black, five Gold, one Black (etc.). Before passing your
needle through all 36 beads again, pass it through the open centers of two side-
by-side hexagons from the first small part of the Black sphere. Then form the
Gold Foundation Ring around the two Black hexagons.

*The Gold Foundation Ring loops
through two Black hexagons.*

Complete the Gold hexagon as before. Rotate your work through the Black hexagons as needed to reach all the parts.

Completed Gold hexagon entangled through two black hexagons

Join the Gold hexagon to the first Gold pentagon. The Gold pentagon should be on the underside—the hollow side—of the domed Black shape. Remember to bead a Spine on top of the join. Make sure the Spines are all on the outside of the Gold sphere. The Spines for the Gold sphere are on the opposite side of the Spines for the Black sphere.

*Connect the Gold pentagon to the Gold hexagon on the **underside** of the Black dome.*

The inside of the Black sphere will be facing the inside of the Gold sphere. The Gold pentagon is not entangled through any other shapes, but the five Gold hexagons that are connected to the Gold pentagon are each entangled through the five Black hexagons.

If you place your two hands palms together, and lace the fingers together, you will get a sense of how the two spheres are entangled. If each hand represents a sphere, all the Spines would be beaded on the backs of the hands, not the palms.

Start the second Gold hexagon. Pick up 36 beads for the Foundation Ring in the same pattern as before: five Gold, one Black, five Gold, one Black (etc.). Before passing your needle through all 36 beads again, pass it through the open centers of two side-by-side hexagons from the first part of the Black sphere. One of these two Black hexagons should be one that already has the first Gold hexagon through it, and the other Black hexagon should be the one next to it that does not have a Gold hexagon through it. Then form the Gold Foundation Ring around the two Black hexagons.

Each new Gold hexagon loops through two Black hexagons—one that already has a Gold hexagon, and the one next to it.

Complete the second Gold hexagon as before. Rotate your work as needed to reach all the parts.

Join the second Gold hexagon to the next side of the Gold pentagon. Travel your needle to the correct position to join the second Gold hexagon to the first Gold hexagon. Remember to bead a Spine on top of the join. Make sure the Spines are all on the outside of the sphere.

The tissue is there just to make the structure easier to see.

Bead the remaining three Gold hexagons the same way: each one entangled
through two Black hexagons. Join each Gold hexagon to the Gold pentagon, and
to the previous Gold hexagon. Remember to bead a Spine on top of the join.
Make sure the Spines are all on the outside of the sphere.

After all five Gold hexagons have been beaded entangled through the Black hexagons, bead the remaining shapes to complete half the Black sphere, and the remaining shapes to complete half the Gold sphere. Detailed information on the method for assembling the entire sphere begins on page 201. You will have already completed the sphere assembly up to page 203, and can continue from there.

Bead the remaining half of each sphere, and join them together as described on page 206.

Mystery Weave Bracelet

The Mystery Weave Bracelet is made of two strips of six-sided hexagons, using a Multiple of three. Depending on the design you choose, some of the hexagons are filled, and some are open. One strip of the bracelet is one hexagon longer than the other. One strip will have an even number of hexagons, and one strip will have an odd number of hexagons. The two strips are woven through each other to make a visually complex and flexible bracelet. A wide variety of patterns and designs can be made. The bracelet is about ⅞ inch wide, and can be whatever length you like. A small watch face could be used in place of the center hexagon.

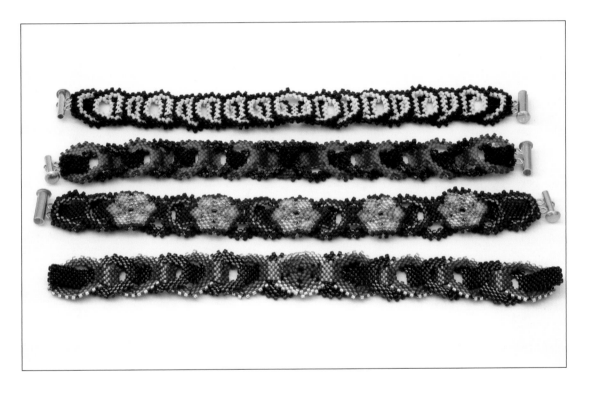

THE MODELS

Shopping

Black and White Model

8 grams Delica 10—Black

9 grams Delica 351—White

Blue Model

8 grams Delica 02 Cut—Metallic

6 grams Delica 748—Dark Blue

4 grams Delica 787—Medium Blue

4 grams Delica 786—Blue Green

Pink Roses Model

9 grams Delica 327—Dark Green

5 grams Delica 690—Moss Green

5 grams Delica 075— Dark Pink

4 grams Delica 071—Light Pink

Rainbow Model

4 grams Delica 602—Red

4 grams Delica 601—Orange

4 grams Delica 145—Yellow

4 grams Delica 148—Green

4 grams Delica 47—Blue

4 grams Delica 610—Purple

Calculating the Foundation Ring

Hexagons: 6 sides x 2 = a Base Number of 12.

The hexagon is made with a Multiple of 3.

Base Number x Multiple = 36, so there are 36 beads in the Foundation Ring of each hexagon.

Techniques in Addition to Basics:

Filled Shapes—see page 31

Flat Odd-Count Peyote Stitch—see page 223

The specific colors and patterns used in the models are detailed on pages 141–145. In the following illustrations, the beads will be shown in different colors to help you tell the rounds apart more easily.

ROUND ONE

All the hexagons in the Mystery Weave Bracelet use a Multiple of three. Pick up 36 beads for the Foundation Ring.

Pass your needle through all 36 beads again, to make a circle. Continue on through a few more beads (it doesn't matter how many) so that your needle is coming out of a different place than your tail.

Leave a tail long enough to sew in later—six or eight inches. You should be beading with a firm, but not tight, tension.

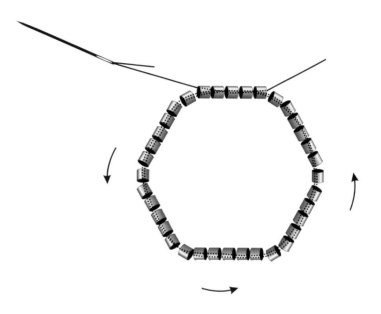

Note: In these illustrations, the Round One beads are represented in red. The specific colors and patterns used in the models are detailed on pages 141–145.

ROUND TWO

Pick up two beads, skip one bead on the Foundation Ring, and stitch through the next bead in the circle.

Pick up one bead, skip one bead on the Foundation Ring, and stitch through the next bead in the circle.

Pick up one bead, skip one bead on the Foundation Ring, and stitch through the next bead in the circle.

Note: In these illustrations, the Round Two beads are represented in yellow. The specific colors and patterns used in the models are detailed on pages 141–145.

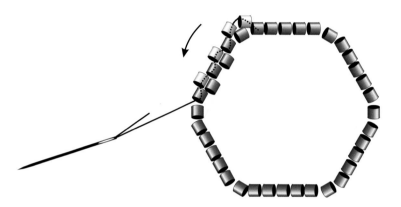

Continue beading around the Foundation Ring in this pattern, adding two beads, then one bead, then one bead, then two beads, until you come around to the beginning. The pairs of beads form the corners of the hexagon.

At the end of this round, after you have added the last single bead, stitch through the first two beads you added in the beginning of this round. This steps up to the next round.

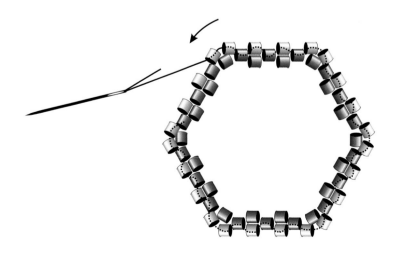

ROUND THREE

Stitch around the hexagon, adding one bead at a time. When you come to the pair of beads that form the corners, pass through them both without adding a bead between them.

At the end of this round, after you have added the last bead, pass your needle through one of the pair of beads. Your needle will come out between the two beads of the pair that forms a corner. Do not step up at the end of Round Three.

Note: In these illustrations, the Round Three beads are represented in green. The specific colors and patterns used in the models are detailed on pages 141–145.

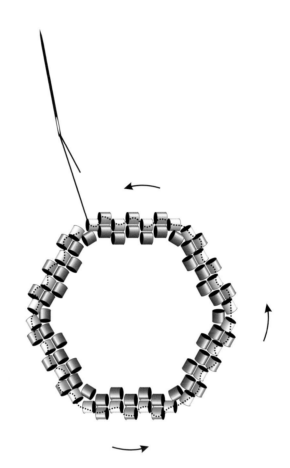

ROUND FOUR

Bead Round Four as detailed on page 9.

Note: In these illustrations, the Round Four beads are represented in blue. The specific colors and patterns used in the models are detailed on pages 141–145.

The First Strip

Bead another hexagon and join it to the first one. Do not bead a Spine on top of the joins. Please see page 15 for more detailed information on joining shapes. The colors of each hexagon, and whether each hexagon is filled or open, will depend on the pattern you are using. The specific colors and patterns used in the models are detailed on pages 141–145.

Please see page 31 for more detailed information on beading filled shapes.

Note: In this illustration, the Joining Row beads are represented in purple. The second hexagon is illustrated as an open hexagon, although it may be open or filled depending on which pattern you are making. The specific colors and patterns used in the models are detailed on pages 141–145. Do not bead a Spine on top of the joins.

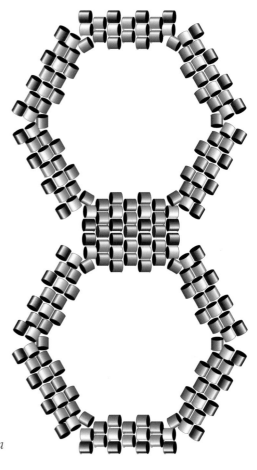

This bracelet is constructed of two strips of hexagons. One strip is one hexagon longer than the other. One strip will have an even number of hexagons, and one strip will have an odd number of hexagons. You will need to decide your desired bracelet length, and bead the longer strip to match that length. Allow for the length of your clasp when calculating the final bracelet length. The odd and even strips will have different patterns, so decide if the longer strip is odd or even. Continue beading and joining either filled or open hexagons, depending on which pattern you are using, until your first strip is as long as you want. Do not bead a Spine on top of the joins.

A strip of seven hexagons produces a beaded strip approximately 6 inches long. A strip of eight hexagons produces a beaded strip approximately 6¾ inches long. A strip of nine hexagons produces a beaded strip approximately 7½ inches long.

The illustrations on the following pages show a strip of nine hexagons and a strip of eight hexagons, but the bracelet can be any length, as long as one strip is one hexagon longer than the other. You may have to make some adjustments in the pattern of filled hexagons and open hexagons in a design like Pink Roses to adjust for different lengths.

The Second Strip

Bead a second strip of hexagons, one shorter than your first strip. The colors of each hexagon, and whether each hexagon is filled or open, will depend on the pattern you are using. The specific colors and patterns used in the models are detailed on pages 141–145.

Colors and Patterns

Black and White Model: Open Hexagons
    Round One (Foundation Ring)—White
    Round Two—Black
    Round Three—Black
    Round Four—Black on four sides, White on two opposite sides
    Joining Row—White (join White sides of hexagons)

Black and White Model: Filled Hexagons
    There are no filled hexagons in this model.

Odd and Even Strips
    Odd-numbered strip: all open hexagons
    Even-numbered strip: all open hexagons
    End tabs—Black

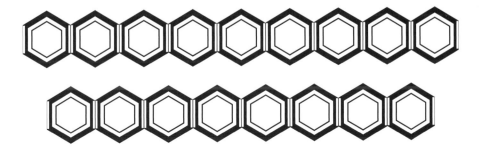

Blue Model: Open Hexagons—Odd-Numbered Strip

Round One (Foundation Ring)—Blue Green
Round Two—Two Dark Blue, one Medium Blue, one Medium Blue, repeat
Round Three—Medium Blue
Round Four—Dark Blue
Joining Row—Dark Blue
End tabs if used on odd strip—Dark Blue

Blue Model: Filled Hexagon—Odd-Numbered Strip

Round One—Blue Green
Round Two—Blue Green
Round Three—Blue Green
Round Four—Blue Green
Round Five—Two-bead-wide sides: Blue Green
Round Six—Two Medium Blue,
        one Blue Green, repeat
Round Seven—Medium Blue
Round Eight—Three-bead-wide sides: Medium Blue
Round Nine—Dark Blue
Round Ten—Dark Blue
Round Eleven—Four-bead-wide sides: Dark Blue
Joining Row—Dark Blue
End tabs if used on odd strip—Dark Blue

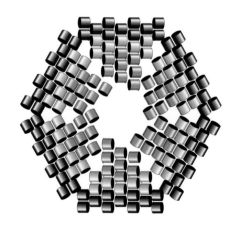

Blue Model: Even-Numbered Strip

All hexagons in even-numbered strip
are open—no filled hexagons
Entire hexagon and joining rows—Metallic
End tabs if used on even strip—Metallic

Odd and Even Strips

Odd-numbered strip: center hexagon is filled
Even-numbered strip: all open hexagons

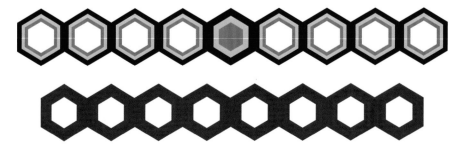

Pink Roses Model: Open Hexagons

Round One (Foundation Ring)—Moss Green
Round Two—Dark Green
Round Three—Dark Green
Round Four—Dark Green
Joining Row—Dark Green

Pink Roses Model: Filled Hexagons

Round One—Dark Pink
Round Two—Dark Pink
Round Three—Dark Pink
Round Four—Light Pink
Round Five—Two-bead-wide sides: Dark Pink
Round Six—Two Dark Pink, one Light Pink, repeat
Round Seven—Light Pink
Round Eight—Three-bead-wide sides: Dark Pink, Light Pink, Dark Pink
Round Nine—Two Dark Green, one Dark Pink, one Dark Pink, repeat
Round Ten—One Dark Pink bead to finish point on petal, one Dark Green,
        one Dark Green, repeat
Round Eleven—Four-bead-wide sides: Dark Green
Joining Row—Dark Green

Filled hexagons have two open hexagons between
them. When one strip is laid on top of the other,
a filled hexagon will sit between two open
hexagons.

Odd and Even Strips

Odd-numbered strip: center hexagon is filled
Even-numbered strip: center two hexagons are open
End tabs on either strip—Dark Green

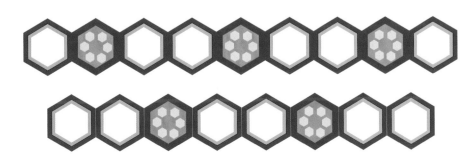

Rainbow Model: Open Red Hexagons

Round One (Foundation Ring)—Red
Round Two—Orange
Round Three—Orange
Round Four—Yellow
Joining Row—Yellow
End tabs if used—Yellow

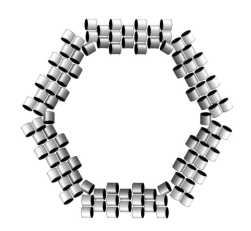

Rainbow Model: Open Blue Hexagons

Round One (Foundation Ring)—Green
Round Two—Blue
Round Three—Blue
Round Four—Purple
Joining Row—Purple
End tabs if used—Purple

Rainbow Model: Filled Red Hexagon

Round One—Red
Round Two—Red
Round Three—Red
Round Four—Red
Round Five—Two-bead-wide sides: Red
Round Six—Two Orange, one Red, repeat
Round Seven—Orange
Round Eight—Three-bead-wide sides: Orange
Round Nine—Yellow
Round Ten—Yellow
Round Eleven—Four-bead-wide sides: Yellow
Joining Row—Yellow

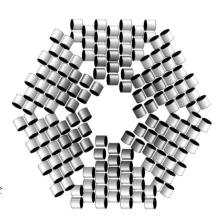

Rainbow Model: Filled Blue Hexagons

Round One—Green
Round Two—Green
Round Three—Green
Round Four—Green
Round Five—Two-bead-wide sides: Green
Round Six—Two Blue, one Green, repeat
Round Seven—Blue
Round Eight—Three-bead-wide sides: Blue
Round Nine—Purple
Round Ten—Purple
Round Eleven—Four-bead-wide sides: Purple
Joining Row—Purple

One strip is all red hexagons, the other strip is all blue hexagons. In the model, the odd-numbered strip is red, and the even-numbered strip is blue. The bracelet can be reversed to show the single center red filled hexagon, or the two center blue filled hexagons.

Odd and Even Strips

Odd-numbered strip: center hexagon is filled
Even-numbered strip: center two hexagons are filled

Beading the End Tabs

One strip is one hexagon longer than the other. The longer strip should be approximately the length of the finished bracelet (minus the clasp length). It doesn't matter if the longer strip is the odd strip or the even strip.

The shorter strip will need to have end tabs beaded onto each side, to make it the same length as the longer strip.

Using peyote stitch, bead additional rows onto the far side of each end hexagon. The end tab will be seven beads wide, and should be about 15 rows long. You should see a total of eight edge beads, including the Round Four bead, on the end tab. The actual length may vary by a row or two—compare your shorter strip of hexagons to the longer strip and bead rows (the same number of rows on each end) until you make the two strips of equal length. The technique to bead the end tab will be just like beading a side of the hexagon—doing Round Three and then Round Four, over and over, on a single side.

Please see page 222 for more detailed information on peyote stitch.

Stop beading each end tab after doing a row of three beads—the row that would be like Round Three.

This end tab is 15 rows long.

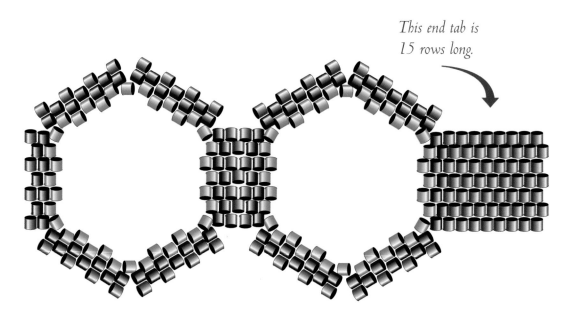

Weaving the Two Strips of Hexagons

The different models have slightly different methods of weaving the two strips together, but the concept is the same for all of them. The strips are passed through each other alternately. Strips are passed underneath filled hexagons.

There are two strips, one of which is one hexagon longer than the other. One strip has an even number of hexagons, and one strip has an odd number of hexagons. In three of the models, the center hexagon of the odd strip is a filled hexagon. In the Black and White model, the center hexagon of the odd strip is open, but it is treated as if it were a filled hexagon.

Lay the two strips together, the odd-numbered strip centered on top of the even-numbered strip. It doesn't matter if the odd-numbered strip is the longer or the shorter of the two strips. The hexagons will not line up, but will be offset from each other.

Look for the open hexagons that are closest to the center of the bracelet. (If you are weaving two strips of open hexagons, as in the Black and White model, treat the center hexagon of the odd strip as if it were filled.) In this example, the open hexagons closest to the center are the red ones on either side of the filled red hexagon.

This red hexagon is closest to the center.

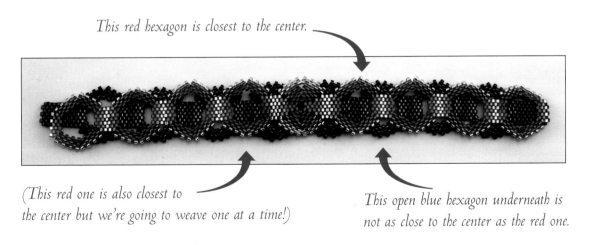

(This red one is also closest to the center but we're going to weave one at a time!)

This open blue hexagon underneath is not as close to the center as the red one.

Pass one end of the bottom strip up through one of the open hexagons closest to the center. You may have to pinch or twist it a little to get it through.

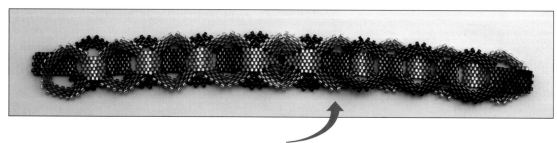

The blue strip has been passed up through the open red hexagon closest to the center.

Pass the other end of the bottom strip up through the open hexagon on the other side of the center.

The blue strip has been passed up through the open red hexagon closest to the center on the other side.

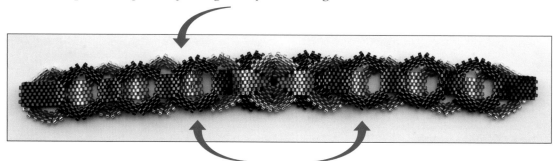

These blue hexagons are now the open hexagons closest to the center.

Notice that the two open hexagons closest to the center are now blue hexagons. Pass the two ends of the lower strip (the red one) up through those two open hexagons.

The red strips have been passed up through the two open blue hexagons.

Continue weaving the strips in this manner. Always look for the open hexagon closest to the center of the bracelet, and pass the other strip through it.

Depending on the design, the open hexagons closest to the center may be on the top strip or the bottom strip. You may be passing the other strip up or down through the open hexagon.

If you miss one of the open hexagons, it'll look like this:

Oops! Missed this one!

Here's what the bracelet looks like reversed:

When you finish weaving the two strips, go back and look for any hexagons you may have missed. When you're sure the weaving is finished, stitch the end tab to the edge of the last hexagon on the other strip, and attach your clasp.

"Look deep into my eyes. Hear my soothing purr. You are getting sleepy. You will go into the kitchen and open a can of tuna..."

Entangled Cubes Necklace

Cubes are made of six square faces. The Entangled Cubes Necklace can be made horizontally or vertically, whichever you choose. Single small cubes would make striking earrings. The cube portion of the necklace is approximately 4 inches wide (or tall).

The horizontal Red-Orange and Green Entangled Cubes Necklace uses two small cubes, one on each end, and one large cube in the center. The vertical Blue-Green and Gold Entangled Cubes Necklaces uses one small cube on the top, one medium cube in the center, and one large cube on the bottom.

The small cube uses a Multiple of five.
The medium cube uses a Multiple of six.
The large cube uses a Multiple of seven.

THE MODELS

Shopping—Red-Orange and Green (horizontal) Model
  7 grams Delica 681—Yellow
  12 grams Delica 43—Orange
  6 grams Delica 603—Red
  12 grams Delica 46—Green

Shopping—Blue-Green and Gold (vertical) Model
  7 grams Aiko 36—Green
  7 grams Aiko 27BD—Aqua
  7 grams Aiko 28—Blue
  14 grams Aiko 743—Purple
  5 grams Aiko 712—Gold

Calculating the Foundation Ring
  Squares: 4 sides x 2 = a Base Number of 8.
    Small Cube's Square is made with a Multiple of 5.
    Base Number x Multiple = 40, so there are 40 beads
    in the Foundation Ring of each small square.
    Medium Cube's Square is made with a Multiple of 6.
    Base Number x Multiple = 48, so there are 48 beads
    in the Foundation Ring of each medium square.
    Large Cube's Square is made with a Multiple of 7.
    Base Number x Multiple = 56, so there are 56 beads
    in the Foundation Ring of each large square.

Techniques in Addition to Basics:
  Making Different Shapes *(squares)*—see page 24
  Making Different Sizes—see page 27
  Linking and Entangling Shapes—see page 65
  Pinching and Attaching Shapes—see page 69
  Flat Odd-Count Peyote Stitch—see page 223
  Tubular Ndbele Stitch—see page 225

A cube is made of six square faces. We're going to bead half a cube at a time. Half a cube consists of three square faces arranged like a little pyramid, forming a point. It's easier to entangle portions of the cubes before the two halves are joined.

The following instructions describe the construction of the vertical Blue-Green and Gold version of the Entangled Cubes Necklace. The slight changes that would produce the horizontal Red-Orange and Green version appear at the end of this project section.

The First Square of the Small Cube

ROUND ONE

The small cube is made of six squares with a Base Number of eight and a Multiple of five, requiring 40 beads in the Foundation Ring. Pick up 40 Green beads.

Pass your needle through all 40 beads again, and through a few more, to make a circle.

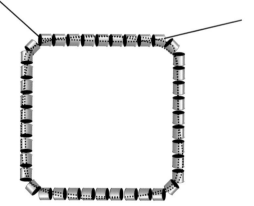

Leave a tail long enough to sew in later—six or eight inches. You should be beading with a firm, but not tight, tension.

ROUND TWO

Pick up two Aqua beads, skip one Green bead on the circle, and stitch through one Green bead on the circle.

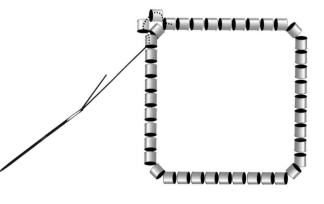

Make four more single
stitches using one Aqua
bead at a time. This will
complete one side of
the square.

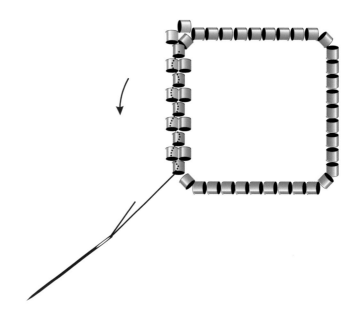

Continue beading the remaining three sides of the square in the same pattern: two
Aqua beads, four stitches of one Aqua bead at a time, two Aqua beads, four
stitches of one Aqua bead at a time, etc.

At the end of this
round, after you have
added the last Aqua
bead, stitch through
the first two Aqua
beads you added in
the beginning of this
round. This steps up
to the next round.

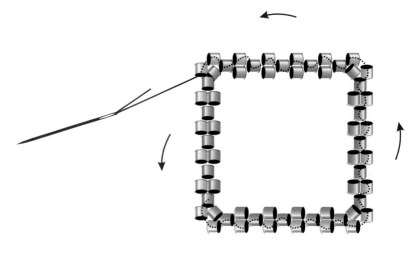

ROUND THREE
Use Blue beads for Round Three.

Stitch around the square, adding one Blue bead at a time. When you come to the pair of beads that form the corners, pass through them both without adding a bead between them.

At the end of this round, after you have added the last Blue bead, pass your needle through one of the pair of Aqua beads from Round Two. Your needle will come out between the two beads of the pair that forms a corner. Do not step up at the end of Round Three.

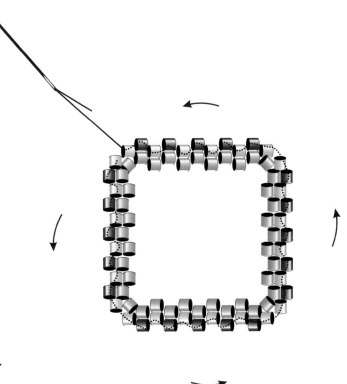

ROUND FOUR
Bead Round Four, using Purple beads, as detailed on page 9.

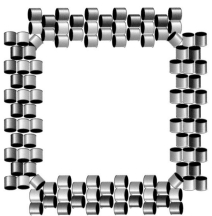

A Multiple of five means there will be six beads on each finished side in Round Four.

Constructing Half the Small Cube

We're going to bead half a cube, then bead half of the next cube entangled through the first half.

Bead a second square, exactly the same as the first one, using a Multiple of five and a Foundation Ring of 40.

Join the second square to the first square. Use Purple beads for the Joining Row. Bead a Spine at the join. Use Gold beads for the Spine.

Note: In the illustration to the right, the Spine is not shown.

Pinch the two squares together and stitch a Round One (Green) bead located near the center of a side of one square to the corresponding Round One bead on the other square.

Please see pages 15–20 for more information on joining shapes and beading Spines.

Please see page 69 for more information on pinching and attaching shapes together.

Note: In the illustration to the right, the pinching of the two squares is not shown.

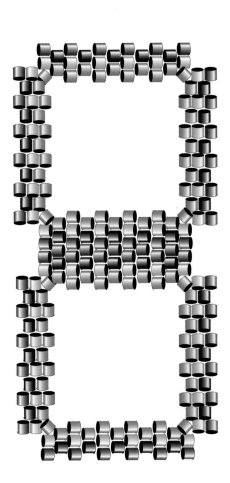

Make another identical square and join it to the next side of the first square. Use the same method you used before, including beading a Spine and pinching and attaching the two sides together. The three joined squares form a small pyramid.

After you join the third square to the first square, travel your needle to the correct

position and join the two adjacent sides of the second and third squares. Every time you join shapes together, bead a Spine on top of the join and pinch and attach the sides together. Make sure the Spines are all on the outside of the cube.

The three squares form half of a small-sized cube. Notice that three sides are joined, as well as three squares. Each joined side has a Spine and is pinched and attached together.

The Second Cube—Entangling with the First Half-Cube

We will bead half of a medium cube with a Multiple of six. There will be 48 beads in the Foundation Ring. Each of the three square faces will be entangled through two of the square faces of the small half-cube.

Note: If you are beading the horizontal version of this necklace, the second cube will be a large cube beaded with a Multiple of seven. There will be 56 beads in the Foundation Ring.

Pick up 48 Green beads. First pass your needle through the open centers of two of the squares of the small half-cube, then pass it through all 48 beads again, to make a circle. Continue on through a few more beads (it doesn't matter how many) so that your needle is coming out of a different place than your tail.

The tail doesn't show in this photo.

Finish beading the medium square, rotating it through the two square faces of the small half-cube as needed to reach all the parts.

Use the same colors as the small squares— Green for Round One, Aqua for Round Two, Blue for Round Three, Purple for Round Four.

Notice that the first square face of the medium cube goes through two square faces of the small cube. It loops around one of the joined sides between two squares. This medium square is entangled through two faces of the small half-cube.

A square with a Multiple of five has six beads on each finished side.

A square with a Multiple of six has seven beads on each finished side.

Bead a second medium square, entangled through two faces of the small half-cube. Don't use the same two faces as the first medium square.

Join the two medium squares together with a Joining Row and a Spine. When you bead the Spine, make sure to orient the two entangled cubes so that the Green beads from one cube are closest to the Green beads of the other cube. Pinch and attach the sides of the two medium squares. Make sure the Spines are all on the outside of the cube.

These two sides have been pinched and attached.

Bead a third medium square, entangled through the two remaining squares of the small half-cube. Join it to the first two medium squares to form half a medium cube. Make sure to attach it to both the first and the second medium square, and to bead a Spine for each join. Pinch and attach each pair of sides together. Make sure the Spines are all on the outside of the cube.

You now have two half-cubes entangled together—one small half and one medium half. Construct another small half-cube with a Multiple of five. Align the two halves of the small cube and join them together, beading a Spine for each join, and pinching and attaching each pair of sides together as they are joined. This completes the small cube, and the medium cube is half complete.

The Third Cube—Entangling with the Second Half-Cube

Bead another medium half-cube with a Multiple of six. Bead half the large cube (with a Multiple of seven) entangled through the faces of the medium half-cube. Remember to bead a Spine for each join, and pinch and attach each pair of sides together. Make sure the Spines are all on the outside of the cube.

Join the two halves of the medium cube. Remember to bead a Spine for each join, and pinch and attach each pair of sides together. This completes the medium cube, and the large cube is half complete.

Bead another large half-cube, and join it to the first half of the large cube.

Note: If you are beading the horizontal version of this necklace, the third cube will be a small cube beaded with a Multiple of five. There will be 40 beads in the Foundation Ring.

Beading the Necklace Bail at the Top

At the top corner of the small cube, pass your needle through the Gold beads that form the Spine, coming out in the gap at the top corner. Add three Gold beads, and stitch into some of the Gold Spine beads directly across the gap, on the same square face.

Turn and stitch back
through all three new
Gold beads, and into some
of the Gold Spine beads
on the other side, to
reinforce the attachment.

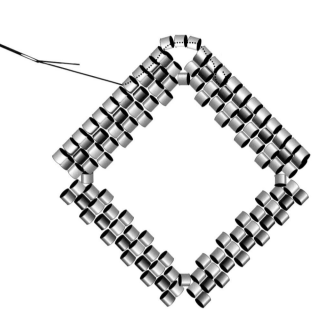

Bead a strip of flat, odd-count peyote stitch three
beads wide, using Gold beads, on top of these three
Gold beads. When it is finished, curl the end around
to the beginning and stitch it securely to the first row
to make a loop. Make the strip long enough to fit
whatever chain or beaded strip you are going to use
for a necklace. In the model, a 24-inch chain of
tubular ndbele stitch, two stitches in diameter, using
Purple beads, was used. I attached a clasp directly
to the ends. A peyote strip of 26 rows (13 edge
beads) fit around this chain.

Please see page 223 for detailed
information on peyote stitch.

Please see page 225 for detailed
information on tubular ndbele stitch.

The Horizontal Red-Orange and Green Entangled Cubes Necklace

The horizontal version of the Entangled Cubes Necklace uses a large cube in the center, with a small cube on either side. Bead these in the same way as detailed in the vertical version's instructions. The small cube uses a Multiple of five and the large cube uses a Multiple of seven. The Foundation Ring of the small cube has 40 beads and the Foundation Ring of the large cube has 56 beads. Use the following colors:

Round One—Yellow
Round Two—Orange
Round Three—Orange
Round Four—Red
Joining Rows—Red
Spine—Green

In the model, I stitched a tubular ndbele chain, two stitches in diameter, using Green beads, directly to each outermost corner of the smallest cubes. Each half was about ten inches long. I attached a clasp directly to the ends.

Please see page 225 for detailed information on tubular ndbele stitch.

Emmett inspects the quality of his mother's hard work.

Seven Cubes Necklace

The Seven Cubes Necklace is a variation of the Entangled Cubes Necklace. I recommend that you become familiar with the construction technique for the Entangled Cubes before you attempt this necklace. These instructions describe only the specific differences between this and the Entangled Cubes Necklace. The largest of the seven cubes is in the center, and the cubes get smaller and smaller going out to the edges. The cubes portion of the necklace is approximately 7 inches long.

The largest center cube is made with a Multiple of seven. The cubes get progressively smaller, using Multiples of six, five, and four.

Cubes are made of six square faces. The Seven Cubes Necklace can be worn horizontally or vertically, whichever you choose. Single small cubes would make striking earrings.

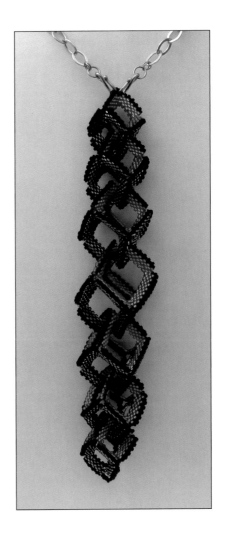

THE MODELS

Shopping
 6 grams Delica 603—Red
 6 grams Delica 601—Orange
 6 grams Delica 681—Yellow
 6 grams Delica 46—Green
 6 grams Delica 608—Blue
 6 grams Delica 610—Purple
 10 grams Delica 10—Black

Calculating the Foundation Rings
 Squares: 4 sides x 2 = a Base Number of 8.

 Small Cube's Square is made with a Multiple of 4.
 Base Number x Multiple = 32, so there are 32 beads
 in the Foundation Ring of each small square.

 Medium-Small Cube's Square is made with a Multiple of 5.
 Base Number x Multiple = 40, so there are 40 beads in the
 Foundation Ring of each medium-small square.

 Medium-Large Cube's Square is made with a Multiple of 6.
 Base Number x Multiple = 48, so there are 48 beads in the
 Foundation Ring of each medium-large square.

 Large (center) Cube's Square is made with a Multiple of 7.
 Base Number x Multiple = 56, so there are 56 beads in the
 Foundation Ring of each large square.

Techniques in Addition to Basics:
 Making Different Shapes *(squares)*—see page 24
 Making Different Sizes—see page 27
 Linking and Entangling Shapes—see page 65
 Pinching and Attaching Shapes—see page 69
 Flat Odd-Count Peyote Stitch—see page 223
 Tubular Ndbele Stitch—see page 225

The First Half of the Large Cube

We will bead half of the large cube first. Bead a Red square, using a Multiple of seven. Pick up 56 beads for the Foundation Ring. Use Red for all four rounds.

Bead an Orange square with a Multiple of seven. Join it to the Red square using Black beads for the Joining Row and Black beads for the Spine.

Please see pages 15–20 for more detailed information on joining shapes and beading Spines.

Pinch and attach the two sides, joining a Round One bead from one square to a Round One bead in the same position on the other square.

Please see page 69 for more detailed information on pinching and attaching shapes.

These two squares have been pinched and attached.

Bead a Yellow square with a Multiple of seven. It is very important to place the Yellow square on the correct side of the Red and Orange squares. Hold the joined Red and Orange squares with the Black Spine facing you. Arrange them so the Red square is on top and the Orange square is on the bottom. Join the Yellow square to the left side of the Red square, and to the left side of the Orange square.

Use Black beads for the Joining Row, and use Black beads for the Spines. Pinch and attach each edge as you attach it to another square.

Clockwise from the corner point of the three square faces, where all three come together, you should see Red, then Orange, then Yellow.

The Medium-Large Cube—Entangling with the Large Cube

Begin beading a medium-large square. This square has a Multiple of six. Pick up 48 Green beads and form the Foundation Ring entangled through the Yellow and Orange squares.

Please see page 65 for more detailed information on entangling shapes.

Please see page 151 for more detailed information on the Entangled Cubes Necklace.

Finish beading the medium-large square using all Green beads.

Bead a Blue square with a Multiple of six entangled through the Red and Yellow squares.

Join the Green square and the Blue square together. Use Black beads for the Joining Row and the Spine. Pinch and attach the two sides together. Make sure that the insides of the two cubes face each other when you join them.

Bead a Purple square with a
Multiple of six entangled through
the Red and Orange squares. Join it
to the Green square and to the Blue
square. Use Black beads for the
Joining Rows and for the Spines.
Pinch and attach two sides together
each time you join them.

Take a moment and notice the
arrangement of these two half-
squares. They form little three-sided
pyramid shapes, with the open parts
facing away from each other.

The Green square is entangled through the Yellow and Orange squares, and is not
touching the Red square.

The Red square is entangled through the Blue and Purple squares, and is not
touching the Green square.

Green and Red are complementary colors. This means they are opposite each
other on a color wheel. They are also opposite each other on this necklace.

Yellow and Purple are also complementary colors. They are opposite each other in
this necklace in the same way as Red and Green. Blue and Orange are also
complementary colors, and are opposite each other on the necklace.

The Second Half of the Large Cube

Bead the second half of the large cube. Using a Multiple of seven, bead a Green
square, and then bead a Blue square. Join them using Black beads for the Joining
Row and for the Spine. Pinch and attach the sides together.

Bead a Purple square with a Multiple of seven. It is very important to place the
Purple square on the correct side of the Green and Blue squares. Hold the joined
Green and Blue squares with the Black Spine facing you. Arrange them so the

Green square is on top, and the Blue square is on the bottom. Join the Purple square to the right side of the Green square, and to the right side of the Blue square.

Use Black beads for the Joining Row, and use Black beads for the Spines. Pinch and attach each edge as you attach it to another square.

Clockwise from the corner point of the three square faces, you should see Green, then Purple, then Blue.

Entangle the squares of the other medium-large cube through the squares of the second half of the large cube.

Entangle the Red square through the Blue and Purple squares.

Entangle the Orange square through the Purple and Green squares.

Join the Orange square to the Red square and bead a Spine. Use Black beads for the Joining Row and Black beads for the Spine. Make sure the insides of the cubes face each other. Pinch and attach the sides.

Entangle the Yellow square through the Blue and Green squares. Join to the Red and Orange squares, bead Spines, and pinch and attach.

Join the two halves of the large cube to each other. Align the colors so that Red is on the opposite side of the cube from Green, so that Orange is on the opposite side of the cube from Blue, so that Yellow is on the opposite side of the cube from Purple.

This large cube is the center of the necklace.

The Medium-Small and Small Cubes—Entangling Them with the Others

Continue beading the necklace in this manner. Each cube has a Red-Orange-Yellow half, and a Green-Blue-Purple half. First bead a free half-cube in the opposite colors of an entangled half that is already beaded. Then bead half the next smaller size of cube entangled through it. Then join the larger half-cube to the other half of the same size.

Each cube has one square face of each color: Red, Orange, Yellow, Green, Blue, and Purple. All Joining Rows are Black. All Spines are Black. All joined squares should be pinched and attached together.

When beading a free half-cube of Red-Orange-Yellow, bead and join the Red square and the Orange square first. Hold them so the Spine is facing up, and so the Red square is above, the Orange square is below. Join the Yellow square to the left side of the Red square and the left side of the Orange square.

Clockwise from the corner point of the three square faces, where all three come together, you should see Red, then Orange, then Yellow.

When entangling squares through a Red-Orange-Yellow half cube, use the following pattern:

> Form the Green square entangled through the Orange and Yellow squares.
> Form the Blue square entangled through the Red and Yellow squares.
> Form the Purple square entangled through the Red and Orange squares.

Make sure that the insides of the two cubes face each other when you join them.

When beading a free half-cube of Green-Blue-Purple, bead and join the Green square and the Blue square first. Hold them so the Spine is facing up, the Green square is above, and the Blue square is below. Join the Purple square to the right side of the Green square and the right side of the Blue square.

Clockwise from the corner point of the three square faces, where all three come together, you should see Purple, then Blue, then Green.

When entangling squares through a Green-Blue-Purple half-cube, use the following pattern:

Form the Red square entangled through the Blue and Purple squares.
Form the Orange square entangled through the Green and Purple squares.
Form the Yellow square entangled through the Green and Blue squares.

When you join the two halves of a cube to each other, align the colors so that Red is on the opposite side of the cube from Green, Orange is on the opposite side of the cube from Blue, and Yellow is on the opposite side of the cube from Purple.

The second halves of the small cubes are not entangled, they simply close off.

Finishing the Necklace

We are going to build a small strip of Black beads at the outer corners of the small cubes. A length of chain with a hook on each end will attach to these strips. To wear the necklace horizontally, hook one end of the chain onto each corner. To wear it vertically, hook both ends of the chain to the same corner.

Bring your needle out of a colored bead that is directly underneath the first Black Spine bead of a join. It can be any one of the three squares that form the outermost corner of the small cube. In this illustration it is a Green bead.

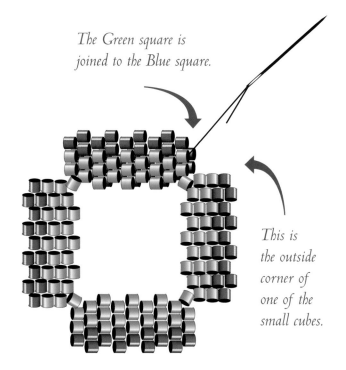

The Green square is joined to the Blue square.

This is the outside corner of one of the small cubes.

Pick up two Black beads. Stitch into the colored bead of the joined square directly underneath the first Black Spine bead. In this illustration it is a Blue bead.

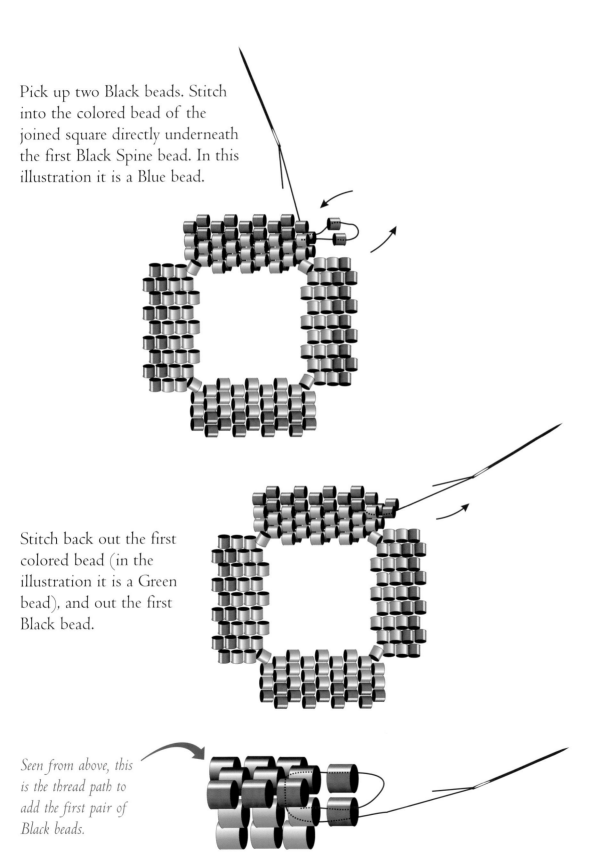

Stitch back out the first colored bead (in the illustration it is a Green bead), and out the first Black bead.

Seen from above, this is the thread path to add the first pair of Black beads.

Continue adding pairs of Black beads in this manner. Pick up two Black beads and loop through the last two Black beads added and out the first Black bead added in this stitch. Add a total of six pairs of beads in this manner.

If your hook is large, you may want to add another row or two to make the end loop a little bigger.

Here are all six pairs of Black beads.

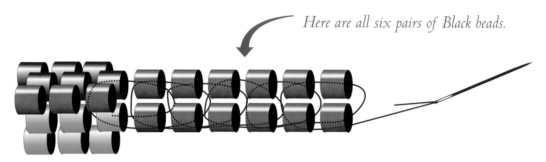

Sew the strip of Black beads to two beads on the opposite end of the cube's corner. The strip makes a little loop by which to attach a hook. You can use a metal chain with a hook at each end, or make a beaded chain with a hook at each end.

To wear the necklace horizontally, hook one end of the chain onto each corner. To wear it vertically, hook booth ends of the chain to the same corner.

Pinched Cube Chain Necklace

Cubes are made of six square faces. Each link of the Pinched Cube Chain Necklace is built on half a cube, or three square faces. Each square face of the half-cube is beaded with a Multiple of five. The beaded portion of the model is approximately 12 inches long.

THE MODEL

Shopping
    41 grams Aiko 706—Green
    13 grams Aiko 712—Gold

Calculating the Foundation Ring
    Squares: 4 sides x 2 = a Base Number of 8.
               The half cube's square is made with a Multiple of 5.
               Base Number x Multiple = 40, so there are 40 beads
               in the Foundation Ring of each square.

Techniques in Addition to Basics:
    Making Different Shapes *(squares)*—see page 24
    Making Different Sizes—see page 27
    Linking and Entangling Shapes—see page 65

We're going to bead half a cube at a time, then entangle another half-cube through it. The edges of the three faces of the half-cube will be brought together and joined to make individual links that are triangular in cross-section. It's not necessary to pinch and attach the sides, as is done in the Entangled Cubes Necklace and the Seven Cubes Necklace.

The First Square of the Cube

ROUND ONE

The half-cube is made of three squares with a Multiple of five, requiring 40 beads in the Foundation Ring. Pick up 40 Green beads.

Pass your needle through all 40 beads again, and through a few more, to make a circle.

Leave a tail long enough to sew in later—six or eight inches. You should be beading with a firm, but not tight, tension.

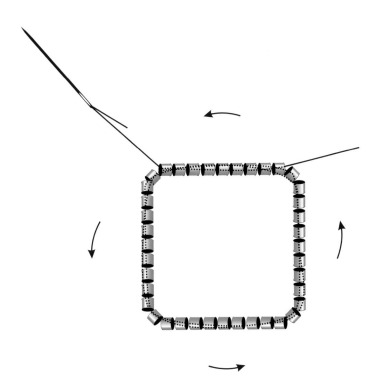

ROUND TWO

Pick up two Green beads, skip one Green bead on the circle, and stitch through one Green bead on the circle.

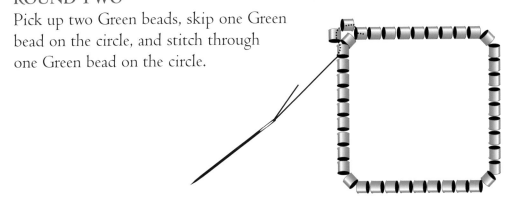

Make four more single stitches using one
Green bead at a time. This will complete
one side of the square.

Continue beading the remaining three sides
of the square in the same pattern: two
Green beads, four stitches of one Green
bead at a time, two Green beads, four
stitches of one Green bead at a
time, etc.

At the end of this
round, after you have
added the last Green
bead, stitch through the first two
Green beads you added in
the beginning of
this round. This
steps up to the next
round.

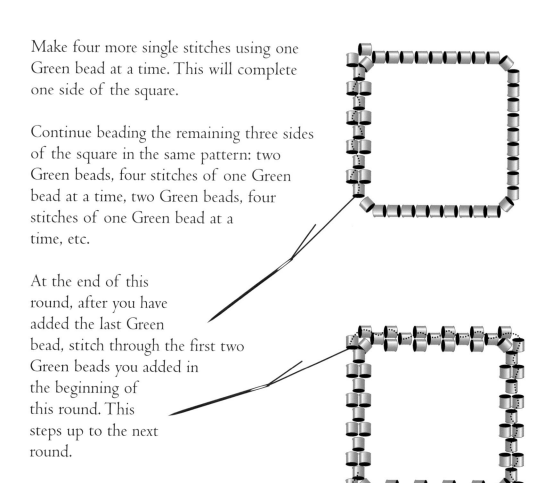

ROUND THREE
Stitch around the square, adding one Green bead at a time.
When you come to the pair of beads
that form the
corners, pass
through them both
without adding a bead
between them.

At the end of this round, after you
have added the last Green bead, pass
your needle through one of the pair
of Green beads from Round Two. Your
needle will come out between the two
beads of the pair that forms a corner. Do
not step up at the end of Round Three.

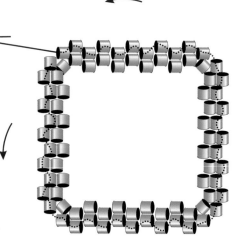

ROUND FOUR

Bead Round Four, using Green beads,
as detailed on page 9.

*A Multiple of five
means there will be
six beads on each
finished side in
Round Four.*

Constructing the Link

We're going to bead a link made from half a cube, then bead the next link made
from another half-cube entangled through the first link.

Bead a second square, exactly the same
as the first one, using a Multiple of five
and a Foundation Ring of 40.

Join the second square to the first square.
Use Green beads for the Joining Row. Bead a
Spine at the join. Use Gold beads for all Spines.

Please see pages
15–20 for more
information on
joining shapes and
beading Spines.

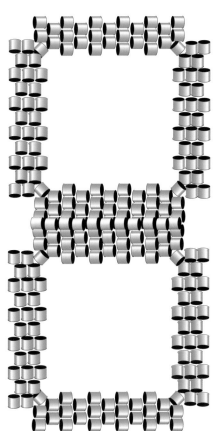

Make another identical square, and join it to the next side of the first square. The three joined squares form a little pyramid.

After you join the third square to the first square, travel your needle to the correct position and join the two adjacent sides of the second and third squares. Every time you join shapes together, bead a Spine on top of the join. Make sure the Spines are all on the outside of the cube.

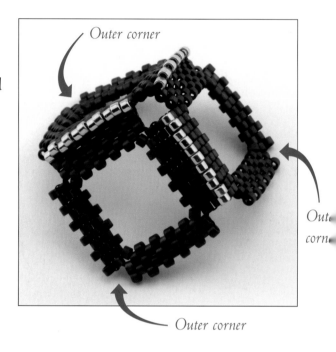

Outer corner

Outer corner

Out... corn...

The three squares form half of a cube. Notice that three sides are joined, as well as three squares. Each joined side has a Spine. Notice the outer corners of each square—the corners that are not attached to anything else.

Bring the outer corners together, squashing the half-cube into a triangular, diamond-shaped object.

Join the sides that have been brought together and bead Spines on top of the joins. This completes one link of the Pinched Cube Chain. Notice that two sides of each square lie next to each other, forming three L-shaped arms of the link.

The Second Half-Cube—Entangling with the Previous Link

We will bead another half-cube, also with a Multiple of five. Each of the three square faces will be entangled through one arm of the first link. The arms of the link were formed of two of the joined square faces of the first half-cube.

Pick up 40 Green beads. First pass your needle through one arm of the first link, then pass it through all 40 beads again, to make a circle. Continue on through a few more beads (it doesn't matter how many) so that your needle is coming out of a different place than your tail.

The tail doesn't show in this photo.

Finish beading the square, rotating it through the arm of the first link as needed to reach all the parts.

Bead another square entangled through a different arm of the first link.

Join these two squares and bead a Spine. Bead a third square entangled through the arm of the first link that does not already have a square entangled through it. Join this square to the first two squares to form a half-cube. Squash this half-cube into a link and join all the edges. Bead Spines on all joins.

Finishing the Necklace

Continue adding links until the chain is as long as you want.

If you are making this Pinched Cube Chain to wear as a necklace, I think it looks nice to bead a smaller link—using a Multiple of four—on each end of the chain as a visual transition. Then bead a smaller link with a Multiple of three entangled through the link with the Multiple of four. Two links don't fit through the hole of a link with a Multiple smaller than four, but the smallest link can be attached to a clasp or metal chain.

In the model, I attached a chain to the smallest link on each end using two pairs of 10mm jump rings on each end, each pair going through one arm of the smallest link. Two of the three arms of the smallest beaded link were attached to the chain with the jump rings.

I used a hook at the end of one length of chain, and left the other length long, so the hook could attach to any point. This makes the necklace adjustable, according to what kind of neckline you are wearing. I beaded a single small link with a Multiple of three and attached it in the same way—with two pairs of jump rings—to the end of the longer piece of chain as an accent to dangle down the back.

Byzantine Chain Necklace

The Byzantine Chain Necklace is constructed with small linked hexagons using a Multiple of two. The beaded portion of the model is approximately 20 inches long.

The necklace consists of segments of pairs of linked Gold hexagons alternating with segments of aqua and blue hexagons in a Byzantine chain pattern. You can vary this any way you like.

THE MODELS

Shopping
17 grams Aiko 27BD—Aqua
12 grams Aiko 28—Blue
32 grams Aiko 712—Gold

Calculating the Foundation Ring
Hexagons: 6 sides x 2 = a Base Number of 12.
The hexagon is made with a Multiple of 2.
Base Number x Multiple = 24, so there are 24 beads
in the Foundation Ring of each hexagon.

Techniques in Addition to Basics:
Linking and Entangling Shapes—see page 65

The hexagons in this necklace are beaded with Rounds One, Two, and Three only. Round Four, which produces the angled sides, is not beaded. Pairs of hexagons will be beaded linked though pairs of other hexagons.

The First Segment of Gold Links

ROUND ONE
Pick up 24 Gold beads.

Pass your needle through all 24 beads again, and through a few more, to make a circle.

Leave a tail long enough to sew in later— six or eight inches. You should be beading with a firm, but not tight, tension.

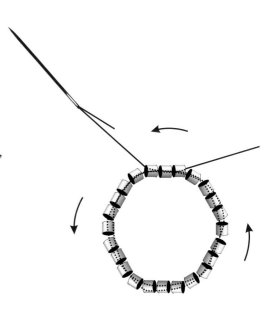

ROUND TWO

Pick up two Gold beads, skip a Gold bead on the circle, and stitch through one Gold bead on the circle. Then pick up one Gold bead, skip a Gold bead on the circle, and stitch through one Gold bead on the circle.

Continue in this pattern all the way around the circle: add two Gold beads, then one Gold bead, then two Gold beads. You will do this a total of six times to come around to the beginning of the circle.

At the end of this round, after you have added the last single Gold beads, stitch through the first two Gold beads you added in the beginning of this round. This steps up to the next round.

ROUND THREE

Using all Gold beads, stitch around the circle, adding one bead at a time. When you come to the two Gold beads from Round Two, pass through them both without adding a bead between them.

At the end of this round, after you have added the last Gold bead, pass your needle through both of the two Gold beads from Round Two. End your working thread and your tail thread by stitching through previous beadwork. There is no Round Four in the hexagons of this necklace. Please see page 13 for more detailed information on ending threads.

Continuing the Chain

Make another identical Gold hexagon. Lay the two Gold hexagons together, one on top of the other.

Begin another identical Gold hexagon by picking up 24 Gold beads. Pass your needle through the open centers of the two previous Gold hexagons before passing it again through the 24 beads. This links the new hexagon through the two previous ones. Please see page 65 for more detailed information on linking beaded shapes.

Finish this linked hexagon,
rotating it as needed
to reach the parts.

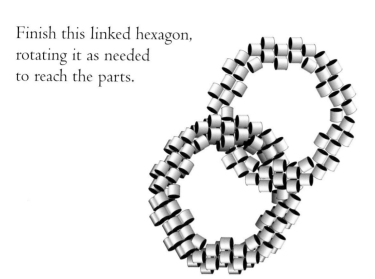

Bead another Gold hexagon
linked through the first two.
The third and fourth hexagons
lie side by side, at right angles
to the first pair of hexagons.

Bead three more pairs of hexagons in this manner, linking each pair to the pair at
the end of the chain. You'll have a total of five pairs of hexagons. This is
sometimes called a Two-In-Two chain.

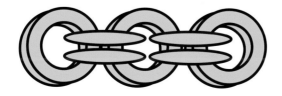

Add a pair of Aqua hexagons to the end of the chain.

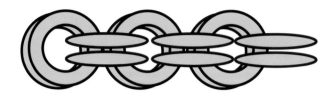

Add a pair of Blue hexagons to the Aqua hexagons at the end of the chain.

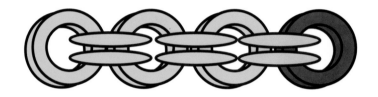

Flip the two Blue hexagons open, like the covers of a book, and fold them back towards the Gold hexagons.

Spread the two Aqua hexagons open in a "V" shape.

Bead two Aqua hexagons linked through the Blue hexagons, between the first two Aqua hexagons.

Add two Blue hexagons linked through the two Aqua hexagons you just beaded.

Add two Aqua hexagons linked through the two Blue hexagons you just beaded.

Flip the two Aqua hexagons open, like the covers of a book, and fold them back towards the previous Aqua hexagons.

Spread the two
Blue hexagons open
in a "V" shape.

Bead two Gold
hexagons linked
through the Aqua
hexagons, between
the two Blue
hexagons. This
completes a
Byzantine unit.

Add four more pairs of Gold hexagons to the end of the chain. Continue
alternating a Blue and Aqua Byzantine unit with five pairs of Gold hexagons.
Make the necklace as long as you want. In the model, I made seven Byzantine
units, with a five-Gold-pairs segment at each end, for a total length of about 20
inches (plus clasp length). I attached a clasp to the last pair of Gold hexagons on
each end. You can also join the necklace in one continuous length so it slips over
your head. It's easiest to do this in the middle of one of the Gold segments.

Chain Maille Necklace

The Chain Maille Necklace is constructed with a base of joined hexagons made with a Multiple of four, and small hexagons using a Multiple of two. The center segment is about 4½ inches tall, and there are about 20 inches of beaded chain plus clasp in the model.

This design was originally inspired by a beautiful bracelet called North Star, created by Sheri Tarrant of www.jollymollybeads.com.

THE MODEL

Shopping
   9 grams Dark Gray—Delica 306
   30 grams Medium Gray—Delica 336
   28 grams Silver—Delica 35

Calculating the Foundation Rings
   Hexagons: 6 sides x 2 = a Base Number of 12.
            Large Hexagon is made with a Multiple of 4.
            Base Number times Multiple = 48, so there are 48 beads
            in the Foundation Ring of each large hexagon.

            Small Hexagon is made with a Multiple of 2.
            Base Number times Multiple = 24, so there are 24 beads
            in the Foundation Ring of each small hexagon.

Techniques in Addition to Basics:
   Linking and Entangling Shapes—see page 65

All the hexagons in this necklace are beaded with Rounds One, Two, and Three only. Round Four, which produces the angled sides, is not beaded. Small hexagons will be beaded entangled through other larger hexagons.

The necklace consists of a two layers of large hexagons: a base of twelve large joined hexagons, and a layer of identical large unjoined hexagons laid on top. All the hexagons of these two layers are connected with pairs of small hexagons entangled through large hexagons on all the joined sides.

The Layer of Joined Hexagons

ROUND ONE

Pick up 48 Dark Gray beads. Pass your needle through all 48 beads again, and through a few more, to make a circle.

Leave a tail long enough to sew in later—six or eight inches. You should be beading with a firm, but not tight, tension.

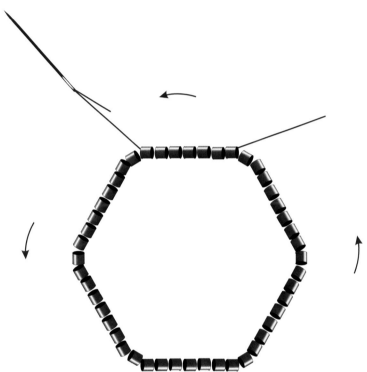

ROUND TWO

Pick up two Medium Gray beads, skip a Dark Gray bead on the circle, and stitch through one Dark Gray bead on the circle. Then pick up one Medium Gray bead, skip a Dark Gray bead on the circle, and stitch through one Dark Gray bead on the circle.

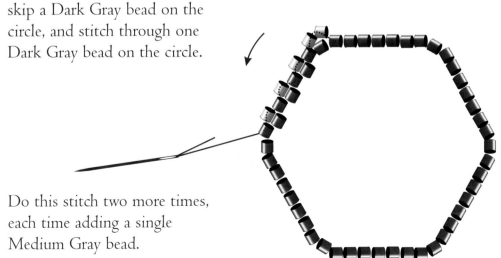

Do this stitch two more times, each time adding a single Medium Gray bead.

Continue in this pattern all the way around the circle: add two Medium Gray beads, then three single stitches of one Medium Gray bead each, then two Medium Gray beads. You will do this a total of six times to come around to the beginning of the circle.

At the end of this round, after you have added the last single Medium Gray bead, stitch through the first two Medium Gray beads you added in the beginning of this round. This steps up to the next round.

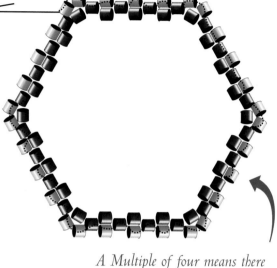

A Multiple of four means there will be three single stitches between corners in Round Two.

ROUND THREE

Using all Medium Gray beads, stitch around the circle, adding one bead at a time. When you come to the two Medium Gray beads from Round Two, pass through them both without adding a bead between them.

At the end of this round, after you have added the last Medium Gray bead, pass your needle through both of the two Medium Gray beads. End your working thread and your tail thread by stitching through previous beadwork. There is no Round Four in any of the hexagons of this necklace. Please see page 13 for more detailed information on ending threads.

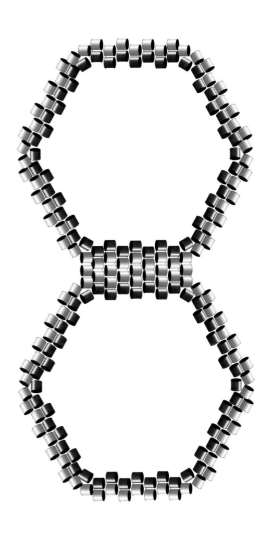

Bead another identical hexagon, and join it to the first one. Use Medium Gray beads for the Joining Row. Please see page 21 for more detailed information on joining shapes with three rounds.

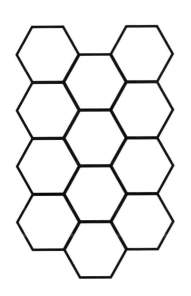

Bead ten more identical hexagons, joining them together in the pattern shown on the left. Most of the hexagons will need to be joined on more than one side.

The Layer of Unjoined Hexagons

Bead twelve more identical hexagons without joining them. End your working thread and tail thread after each hexagon. Please see page 13 for more detailed information on ending threads.

Lay one hexagon on top of each of the twelve joined hexagons from the previous layer. None of the twelve hexagons from this layer are joined to each other. This second layer of hexagons is not connected to the first layer.

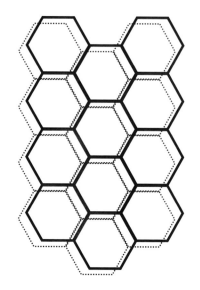

The Small Entangling Hexagons

Pick up 24 Medium Gray beads.

Pass your needle through the open centers of four of the large hexagons: two that are joined together in the first layer, and the two unjoined ones in the second layer on top. Then pass it through the 24 Medium Gray beads, and through a few more, to form a circle, so your tail is not coming out of the same place as your working thread. This entangles the new small hexagon through the previous large ones. Please see page 65 for more detailed information on entangling beaded shapes.

Note: In the illustration to the right, the Foundation Ring of the small hexagon is shown in yellow, to make it easier to see.

The Foundation Ring of the small hexagon is really Medium Gray.

Finish this entangled hexagon, rotating it as needed to reach the parts. Use Silver beads for Round Two and Round Three.

Note: In these illustrations, the small hexagons are shown in yellow, to make them easier to see.

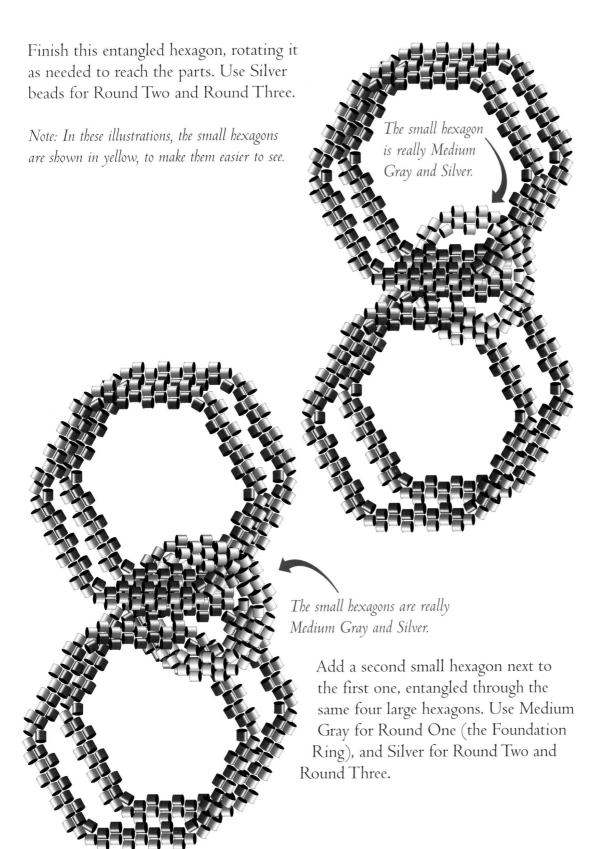

The small hexagon is really Medium Gray and Silver.

The small hexagons are really Medium Gray and Silver.

Add a second small hexagon next to the first one, entangled through the same four large hexagons. Use Medium Gray for Round One (the Foundation Ring), and Silver for Round Two and Round Three.

Continue to entangle two small hexagons through four large hexagons—two joined large hexagons from the first layer, and two loose, unjoined hexagons from the second layer—everywhere there was a join in the first layer. The pattern formed is shown on the right. The locations of the small hexagons are represented as red lines in the illustration.

This pattern is a form of chain maille also known as the Japanese Six-In-One. Many other forms of chain and chain maille can be done in beadwork with this method.

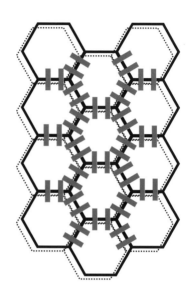

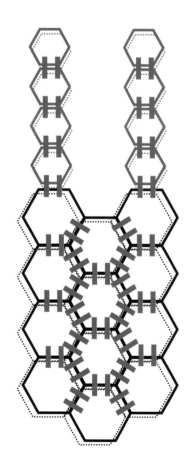

For a chain to go around your neck, link a pair of small hexagons through the top pair of large hexagons. Continue linking two small hexagons through the previous two until the necklace is as long as you like. This form of chain is sometimes called a Two-In-Two. You can connect the two sides so the necklace slips over your head, or attach a clasp. In the model, I beaded 27 pairs of small hexagons on each side, making a length of approximately 10 inches of chain on each side, and attached each end to a clasp. The central unit of chain maille is about 4½ inches long.

Sphere Assembly

Several projects in this book—Star Sphere (page 79), Three Ivory Spheres (page 85), Rainbow Sphere (page 93), and Entangled Spheres (page 123) use the same assembly method. Not to get too technical on you, but that kind of sphere is called a truncated icosahedron, one of the thirteen regular Archimedean solids. It is made of 12 five-sided pentagons and 20 six-sided hexagons. A traditional soccer ball is another example of this same sphere. It's also known as a Buckyball.

There are many different spheres, using different shapes. A couple of examples are Stars and Stripes Forever (page 101), which is a dodecahedron, and Octagon Sphere (page 109), which is a great rhombicuboctahedron (whew!). However, the four projects mentioned in the first paragraph are all assembled using the following method.

We bead this form of sphere one half at a time, then connect the two halves. Imagine that when you bead the first half, you are beading the top half of a globe, with the North Pole at the center. When you bead the second half, you are beading the bottom half of a globe, with the South Pole at the center. When you join the two halves, you are joining them around the equator.

Beading half the sphere starts with a five-sided pentagon. This shape will be at the North Pole of your half sphere. (Please see page 24 for more detailed information on beading shapes.)

Note: In these illustrations, the photos show pentagons and hexagons made into stars. Please see page 39 for more detailed information on making shapes into stars.

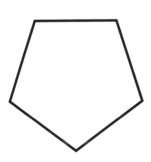

Make a six-sided hexagon and join it to one side of the first pentagon. Bead a Spine on top of the join. (Please see pages 15–20 for more detailed information on joining beaded shapes and beading Spines.)

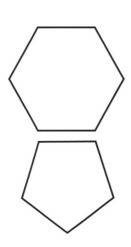

Make another hexagon and join it to the next side of the pentagon. Use the same method as you used before, including making a Spine.

After you join the second hexagon to the pentagon, travel your needle to the correct position and join the two adjacent sides of the two hexagons. Every time you join shapes together, bead a Spine on top of the join. Make sure the Spines are all on the outside of the sphere.

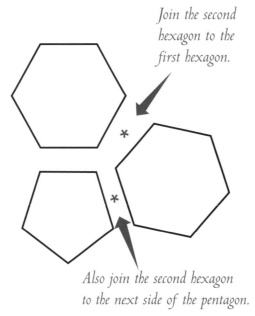

Join the second hexagon to the first hexagon.

Also join the second hexagon to the next side of the pentagon.

Bead three more hexagons and join one to each remaining side of the pentagon. Join each one to the adjacent side of the previous hexagon as well. The fifth hexagon will need to be joined on three sides.

You now have a ring of five hexagons around a single pentagon. The ring forms a little dome. Remember to think of the first pentagon as the North Pole of the half-sphere you are beading.

Be careful where you attach each hexagon—it's easy to get mixed up and attach it between two hexagons, instead of attaching it to a side of the pentagon.

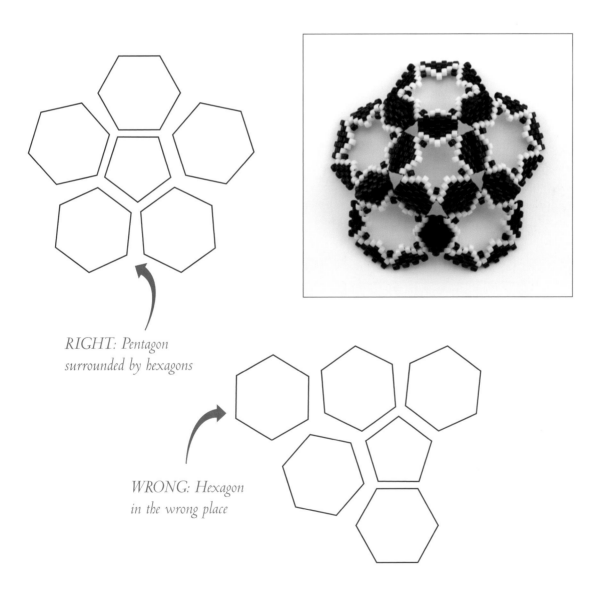

RIGHT: Pentagon surrounded by hexagons

WRONG: Hexagon in the wrong place

Bead five more hexagons and attach one to each hexagon side that is directly opposite the central pentagon. You will join only one side for each hexagon you add. Remember to bead a Spine on top of every join. Make sure the Spines are all on the outside of the sphere.

Bead a pentagon and join it in the deep opening between two of the outermost hexagons. One point of the pentagon should fit into the "V" between two of the innermost hexagons. You will need to join this pentagon on four sides, so make sure to use a longer working thread when constructing these pentagons. Remember to bead a Spine on top of every join. Make sure the Spines are all on the outside of the sphere.

Join each pentagon on four sides.

Bead four more pentagons and join them in the remaining four spaces between the outermost hexagons. When all five pentagons are attached, the beadwork forms a half-sphere.

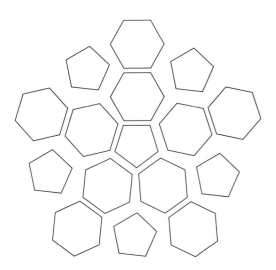

It's very easy to get mixed up on where to attach a pentagon at this point. If you attach a pentagon in the wrong place, there is no way to fix the problem except to remove the pentagon and re-join it. It helps to tie a brightly colored thread to the first, central pentagon to help you keep track of where you are.

Think of the first pentagon as the North Pole, and remember that you are adding pentagons around the equator.

Now you get to go back and do it all again for the other half!

Once you have the two halves of the sphere beaded, you will see that they fit together like two puzzle pieces. The protruding hexagons of one half fit into the recessed pentagons of the other half.

To join the two halves into a sphere, align the halves into the proper orientation, and begin joining sides. Use the same method as you have been using all along, and join each side together around the equator of the sphere. It may help to stuff a piece of fabric inside the two halves to give them some structure as you begin to join them, but don't forget to take it out before you go too far!

The half-spheres will be a little flexible and squashable, but as they are joined together, they firm up and form a self-supporting sphere. A few of the shapes may recede from the surface, but they are easily readjusted by putting a blunt object through a hole and pressing them up from the underside.

PART FOUR

The Gallery

Wendy Hubick
Sue Jackson

Photos: Wendy Hubick

*Wendy and Sue's evening bag is exquisite
in every detail.*

Birgit Bergemann

Birgit's sphere is an amazing accomplishment: she beaded it after seeing a photo of my Star Sphere, without knowing how I had done it. Her technique was completely different from mine!

Photo: Birgit Bergemann

Dottie Bezanilla

Joann Boyer

Photo: Sam Hay

Jennifer Boyle

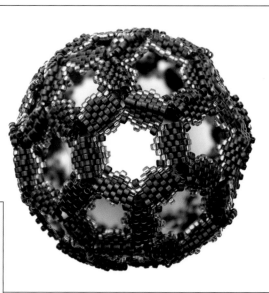

Photos: Ross Paxton

Jennifer's sphere, made entirely of filled shapes, was stiffened by dipping it into floor polish.

Joan Buzecky

Phyllis Dintenfass

Photo: Mark Dintenfass

Notice how Joan and Sue came up with different ways of accenting the stars with crystals.

Sue Doran

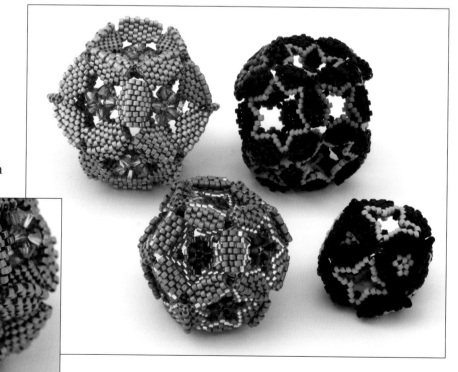

Sandy Houk

Annette Hernandez

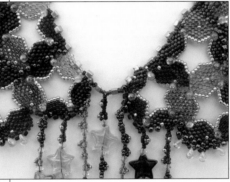

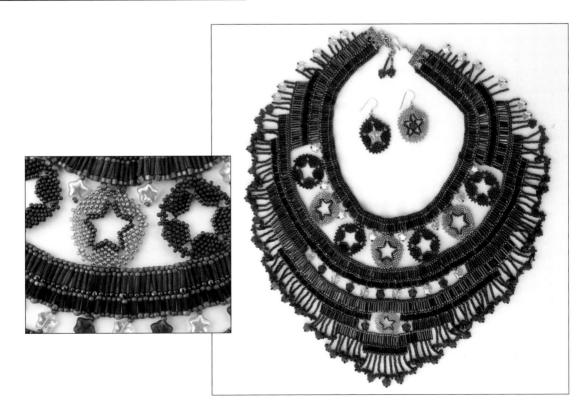

Cathy Mykles

Cathy's version of Three Ivory Spheres took her only two months—she's lots faster than I am!

Photo: Cathy Mykles

Deb Schings

Dichroic coated Aiko beads made a stunning contrast against flat black.

Susan Sneed

Sheri Tarrant

Elizabeth Townes

Table top rivolis were bezeled behind the stars in this little dodecahedron.

Anita Reinehr

Anita Reinehr

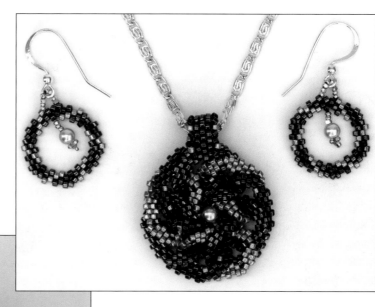

*Anita's elegant variations
are absolutely incredible!*

Judy Walker

This piece was inspired by Scott David Plumlee's "Celtic Design," in his book "Handcrafting Chain and Bead Jewelry."

Emi Yamada

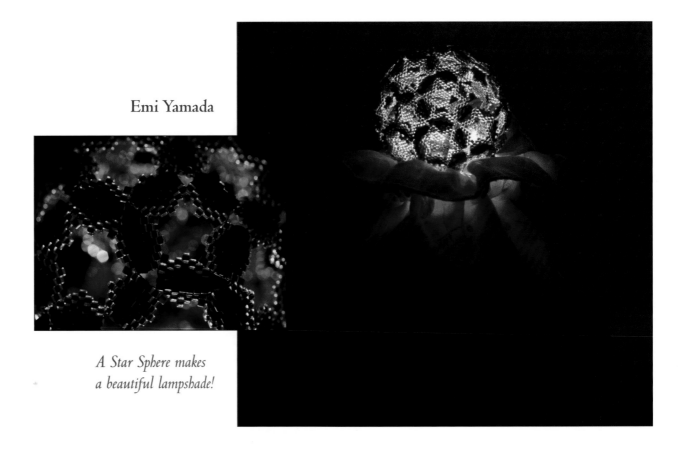

A Star Sphere makes a beautiful lampshade!

Keiko Wada

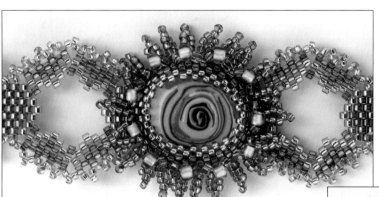

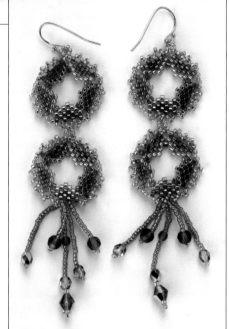

An elegant use of dichroic coated Aiko beads.

Jan Zicarelli

PART FIVE

Additional Information

Stitch Reference

Flat Even-Count Peyote Stitch

A row of peyote stitch has half as many beads as the width of the total project. A ten-bead-wide project has five beads in each row. Each row is half a bead higher than the previous row. When doing flat peyote stitch, you change directions with each row, going back and forth. If it is more comfortable for you, you can turn the work over after each row, so you are always beading in the same direction. Right-handed people tend to be more comfortable beading from right to left.

To start, pick up enough beads for the first two rows. These illustrations show flat even-count peyote stitch, ten beads wide. In this case, the first two rows consist of ten beads, as shown in the illustration below. The beads are numbered in the order you have picked them up on the needle.

For the third row, pick up a single bead, skip a bead, and go through a bead. Repeat these steps until the end of the row. In the illustration below, you have just picked up Bead 14. You would skip Bead 4 and stitch through Bead 3.

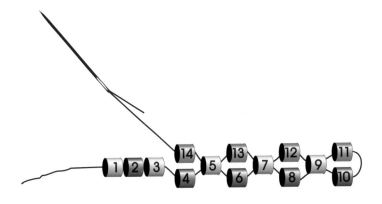

So you can clearly see the thread path, these illustrations show the beads being much more loose than you would really stitch them. In reality, you would pull the thread firmly, but not too tightly, so the beads stack up with the single bead between the pairs of beads. This forms "high beads" and "low beads." In these illustrations, Row One beads are shown in red, Row Two beads in yellow, Row Three beads in green, and Round Four beads in blue.

For all subsequent rows, pick up a bead and go through the next high bead. In the illustration to the right, Bead 16 is the first bead of Row Four. After adding this bead, you would go through Bead 15.

You are always going to be adding a new bead on top of a low bead, and going through a high bead. The new bead you just added becomes the new high bead for the next row, and the bead you went through becomes the new low bead for the next row.

Depending on what is comfortable for you, you might be working from left to right or from right to left. You might be adding beads to the bottom of your work, or you might be adding beads to the top. When doing flat peyote stitch, you may turn your work over at the end of each row. All these ways are right!

Flat Odd-Count Peyote Stitch

Flat odd-count peyote stitch is done in exactly the same way as flat even-count peyote stitch, with one exception. When doing flat odd-count peyote stitch, you need to make a "funny turn" to reposition your needle at the end of every other row—the odd-numbered rows. Without the funny turn, the last bead added will have nowhere to attach. Flat even-count peyote stitch always has a place for the last bead in the row to be attached.

Funny Turn on Odd Rows

In the illustration to the right, you need to add one more bead to finish the row, but there is nowhere to attach it.

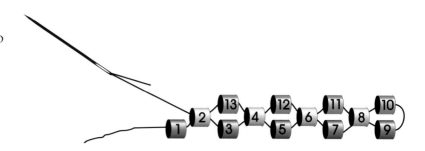

Pass the needle down through the low bead that is a half-bead below the bead you just went through. In the illustration to the right, this is Bead 1. Pick up one bead, which will be the last bead for this row (Bead 14 in this illustration).

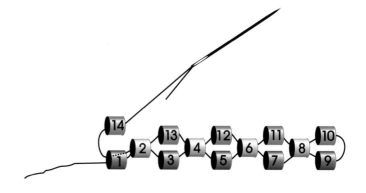

Pass your needle through the bead next to the new bead, and through one more bead. In this illustration, these are Bead 2 and Bead 13.

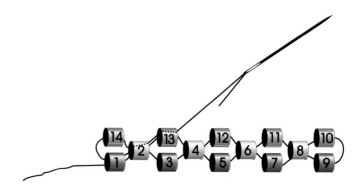

Turn and go through the bead directly below the last bead you just went through. In this illustration, this is Bead 3.

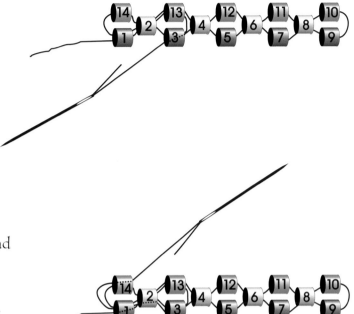

Continue out to the end of the row. In this illustration, you would stitch through Bead 2 and Bead 1, then turn and go through the new bead (Bead 14 in this illustration). Now your thread is in the correct position and you're ready to bead the next row.

In flat odd-count peyote stitch, the funny turn is done at the end of every other row—the odd-numbered rows. In the previous illustrations, the funny turn was done at the end of Row Three. Row Five and Row Seven also need funny turns at the ends, and so on. The even-numbered rows have an even number of sticking-up beads in them, and the odd-numbered rows have an odd number of sticking-up beads in them.

Tubular Ndbele Stitch Two Stitches in Diameter

I often use a small tubular chain of ndbele stitch, two stitches (four beads) around, as a necklace for some of my geometric beadwork. Ndebele stitch lends itself to a tubular form beautifully, making an incomparably flexible slinky tube.

Make a bead ladder with four beads.

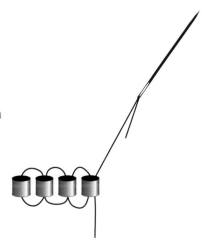

Join the ends in a ring.

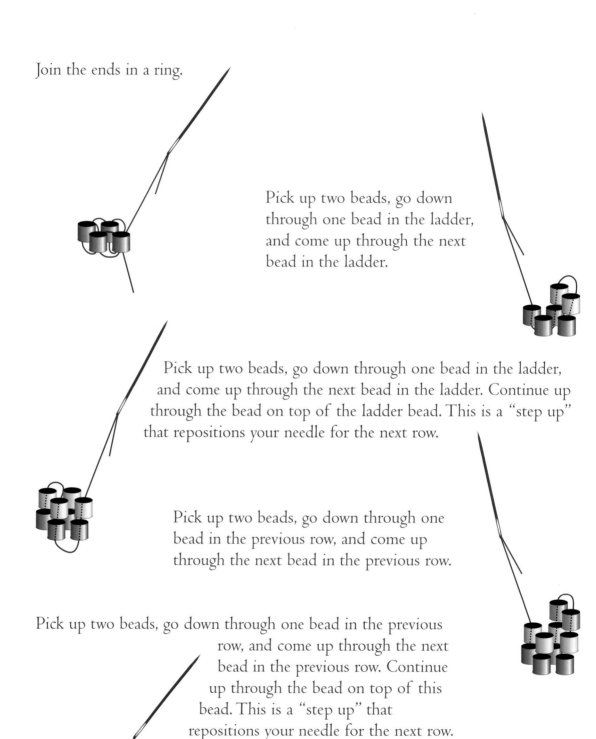

Pick up two beads, go down through one bead in the ladder, and come up through the next bead in the ladder.

Pick up two beads, go down through one bead in the ladder, and come up through the next bead in the ladder. Continue up through the bead on top of the ladder bead. This is a "step up" that repositions your needle for the next row.

Pick up two beads, go down through one bead in the previous row, and come up through the next bead in the previous row.

Pick up two beads, go down through one bead in the previous row, and come up through the next bead in the previous row. Continue up through the bead on top of this bead. This is a "step up" that repositions your needle for the next row.

Continue beading in this manner, adding two beads for each stitch, two stitches for each row. Always step up at the end of every row—after every other stitch of two beads. If you don't, the concentric rows of ndebele will be distorted and become a spiral.

Resources

These are some of my favorite suppliers of the materials I mention in this book.

Miyuki Delica Beads:

    Caravan Beads—www.caravanbeads.net

    Out On A Whim—www.whimbeads.com

    Foxden Beads—www.foxdendesigns.com

    General Bead—www.genbead.com

Toho Treasure and Aiko Beads:

    Tambrook Beads (wholesale only)—www.tambrookbeads.com

    Bobby Beads (wholesale and retail)—www.bobbybead.com

Dichroic Aiko Beads:

    Dichroic Beads By Kawahara—www.dichrobeads.com

Clasps and Findings:

    Rio Grande Jewelry Supply—www.riogrande.com

    Fire Mountain Beads—www.firemountaingems.com

    Rings & Things—www.rings-things.com

    Shipwreck Beads—www.shipwreckbeads.com

Here are some terms to search for on the Internet to get more ideas:

    Platonic solids

    Archimedean solids

    chain mail or chain maille

    quilt blocks

    tile patterns

    polyhedra

    geometric shapes

A Few Words on Copyright

Beading is unusual among art forms, because it's possible—even expected—that beaders will make exact copies of another artist's work. Several excellent magazine articles have been published on copyright from a beader's perspective and lively discussions take place online debating what constitutes a copyright violation in the bead world.

In my opinion, it's not possible for copyright law to address every possible case. If you think about it, all law is an attempt to specify and enforce what we think of as good and courteous behavior. Some aspects of copyright are very clear, and some are in more of a gray area. With cases that fall into that gray area, the ethical thing to do is to make sure you're not violating an artist's wishes. I've found that almost everyone in the bead world tries to do the ethical thing. Sometimes they're not sure what that is, and they can unintentionally cause a lot of pain and unhappiness if they guess. The proper thing to do is ask the artist.

So I thought I'd make my wishes clear. I am honored if you copy my designs bead for bead and color for color. That's why I wrote this book! But I would like those beaded objects to be only for your own use and pleasure.

If you barter, trade, donate, or give one of these designs as a gift, please accompany it, in writing, with the information "An original design by Judy Walker, beaded by (your name).

Please do not make these exact designs for sale. If you develop your own significant variation using these techniques—something different enough so it's clearly not the same as my work—you are welcome to sell that. Simply changing the color or size of my work doesn't make yours different enough.

Please do not enter any of these designs in any contest, show, or exhibit.

If you have any questions, please feel free to contact me. Thank you.

www.walkerpublications.com

Afterword

Many people deserve thanks for their contributions to this book. I've had inspiration and encouragement and help from numerous friends, including Sue Jackson and Wendy Hubick, Huib Petersen, Don Pierce, Laura Shea, Beckah Krahula, and Scott David Plumlee. Carole Sturgis provided invaluable help and support in reading the early manuscript from an accomplished beader's point of view. Brown Balasi's suggestions made the back cover look beautiful. Editor Evelyn Hughes honed the text and provided vital writing suggestions. Art director Claudia Laub did a beautiful job of layout and design on an impossibly tight schedule. Graphic designer Barbara Jefferies took raw text and magically produced the polished and professional book of my dreams. Thank you all, and a big thank-you to all my students throughout the years. I've learned new things from every group I've taught.

I hope you've enjoyed the photos of our cats throughout this book—I would have finished this book a lot sooner without their "help"! (I'm sure many beaders have experienced the feline urge to disrupt beadwork.)

In closing, let me make one pet-related plea—be sure to keep needles and all forms of beading thread away from your pets. Even a few inches of thread can be deadly if it gets into an animal's intestines. I always wrap leftover lengths of thread around my finger and then cut the coil so the thread becomes harmless short lengths. It only takes a moment and can save your pet's life. After all, what would you rather spend money on—a vet emergency room visit or beads?

About the Author

JUDY WALKER I have always loved to bead and I've also practiced many fiber and paper arts. It's intriguing to speculate exactly why an artist develops an intense passion for one specific endeavor, but only beading has all the elements that satisfy my creativity.

Beads are among the oldest of human creations discovered by archeologists, unearthed alongside primitive hunting and warfare tools. Perhaps beads were the first objects created for love of beauty rather than sheer need for survival? Some of that ancient love might be in my hands as I add one bead to the next.

My jewelry and sculpture is rooted in symmetry and precision, expressing through beads the elements of geometry and pattern, of exactness and angle, of illusion and color. Everyday objects provide inspiration—mosaic tiles, an iron fence, Florentine stitchery, an automotive grille, a seed pod, Celtic knotwork—and I imagine those patterns in beads. Slowly, gradually, a unique creation grows from tiny bits of colored glass. Often the piece may look completely different from what I originally had in mind. The beads contain their own surprises and make their own plans.

I love to teach beading, too, and have taught at bead shows, bead stores, music festivals, schools, private classes, and in Japan as a guest of Toho. I've had many wonderful and inspiring students over the years, and always learn as much from them as they do from me. This book grew out of my wish to contribute even more to the art I love so much.

About the Photographer

RICHARD WALKER Witnessing my wife's book steadily progress from initial concept all the way to completion has been a very rewarding experience. My roles were photography and post-processing, making an occasional suggestion, and serving as a sounding board for Judy.

In my own life I've walked varied roads, including citrus ranching, guitar making, writing and publishing books on wood and metalworking, and being a dealer of industrial surplus. I'm privileged to have shared a small part in this book, which will inspire beaders worldwide to explore the techniques and concepts of geometric beadwork.

About the Cats

MOLLY	EMMETT	AMANDA	LUKE	JENNY
Hobbies: panic attacks, princess attitudes, drooling purrs	*Hobbies: hairball formation, drinking from faucets, typing with butt*	*Hobbies: food, naps in sunshine, more food*	*Hobbies: moths on screen doors, chaos, destruction, snuggling*	*Hobbies: bird watching, catnip consumption, lap domination*

The End